The Quarter Horse

The

Quarter Horse

written and illustrated by Walter D. Osborne

Grosset & Dunlap   *Publishers*   New York

1972 Printing

Introduction

This is a book about horses—a particular and unusual breed of horses—and how they came to be as they are today.

From almost the earliest colonial times (both Spanish and British) to the present-day renewal of interest in equestrian activities, no horses have played so prominent a role in the history and folklore of this country as have Quarter Horses and their ancestors. Just as we did ourselves, Quarter Horses evolved and changed with the times, undergoing the mixing of many influences in their blood, until they emerged as a true type—as "typical Americans."

Like every classic family of horses, Quarter Horses are the product of selective breeding.

An intelligent selective breeding program aims at two general qualities: conformation and character. Conformation is, or should be, the physical make-up which enables the animal to do best the job for which he was bred, whether that be to pace between the shafts of a sulky, fly over a seven-foot barrier, or cut a balky steer from a herd of range stock. Character is not only the inbred tendency to excel at one such task, but also the "heart" the horse puts into his work.

The eminent horseman Friedrich Becker once wrote: "A strong mind may master a weak body, but the strongest body will not master a weak mind. . . . The high-spirited horse will always prove a better performer than the physically powerful but low-spirited animal."

The late "Sunny Jim" Fitzsimmons put it more simply when he said, "It is what you can't see that matters."

Certainly the Quarter Horse is most admirably put together physically to do the many jobs which he is called upon to do. But perhaps it is that "unseen" quality that makes him the truly great performer that he is, for in his inborn generosity he has no equal in the horse kingdom.

For newcomers to the wonderful world of Quarter Horses, the author hopes this book will serve at least as an adequate introduction to this most popular of all American horse families. To those already well acquainted with the breed it may possibly bring an even greater enjoyment of their animals through a deeper understanding of their importance in our history and tradition.

More than either of these considerations, though, it has been the writer's wish to capture some of the flavor of that sentiment so ably expressed by Robert J. Kleberg Jr., president of King Ranch and one of the nation's leading breeders of Quarter Horses, when he wrote: "Men may ride hundreds of miles, side by side in an airplane, Pullman or bus and never get past commenting on the weather. . . . But put two men together on horseback, whether on the prairies or the bridle path, and between them there is created a community of spirit that is established and which endures, even if neither speaks a word."

This kinship, born of a common love for our animals, is one which will never be erased by the onslaught of automation or atom-powered machinery. And to it, no animal has contributed in fuller measure than has our native American Quarter Horse.

Numerous individuals and organizations have been of great assistance in the writing of this book. In particular, the author would like to express his thanks to Mr. Roy Davis, editor of the *Quarter Horse Journal* and Mr. Garford Wilkinson, of the American Quarter Horse Association; to Mr. John F. Kennedy, of the Jockey Club; to Mr. Alexander Mackay-Smith, editor of the *Chronicle of the Horse,* and to Mrs. Amelia King Buckley, of the Keeneland Association Library, Lexington, Kentucky, for their invaluable help. Outstanding among the libraries and collections whose facilities were used in its preparation were: The Caroliniana collection of the University of South Carolina; the Sportsman's Library, Middleburg, Virginia; the Hall of the Horsemen, at the Library of the University of Texas, and the New York Public Library. To the always attentive personnel of these institutions, my sincerest gratitude. I would also like to extend special thanks to Mr. Rex C. Cauble, Mr. Buster Welch, and Mr. Dale Wilkinson for the time and effort they spent in providing, not only their personal services, but also many of the outstanding horses which appear in the photographs.

WALTER D. OSBORNE

Contents

The Quarter Horse

Quarter Horses participating in bull-dogging event at the Missoula, Montana, Rodeo.

Why the Quarter Horse?

The United States today is in the midst of the greatest boom in horseflesh it has seen since the invention of the gasoline engine. From fewer than one million pleasure horses in 1945, the number of horses in the country has mounted to today's total of more than six million. And apparently the end is nowhere in sight.

In this great renewal of interest in horses, the American Quarter Horse has taken a commanding lead—and one which keeps increasing with each passing year. From modest beginnings less than three decades ago when the Quarter Horse registry was established, registrations have zoomed to some 60,000 foals a year. This is nearly four times the number recorded annually for Thoroughbreds, the Quarter Horse's nearest rival in popularity; a fact which is all the more astonishing when one considers that Thoroughbred racing is, with nearly fifty million spectators a year, America's largest spectator sport.

Why this heavy swing to this one breed of horse? The reason, I believe, lies in the horse himself, and in the many activities at which he excels over all other horses.

These activities, generally speaking, are not the sort of things the Thoroughbred owner or the master of a harness-racing stable must watch through a set of binoculars while a professional rider or driver puts his animal through its paces. For while it is true that professional Quarter Horse racing is indeed a fast-rising sport, 90 per cent of Quarter Horses are employed in the sort of activities in which the owner and his horse can participate together. These range all the way from the difficult arts of cutting and roping to just simple pleasure riding in the open country. In fact, it can be safely said that there are more different ways in which a Quarter Horse owner can enjoy his horse than there are with any other breed.

11

Thousands of words would be needed to catalogue the physical assets, the virtues of great adaptability and sunny disposition, that, added up, would present a portrait of the modern Quarter Horse. But all of these qualities can be captured in a single word—"companion." Of all the breeds in America today, it is the Quarter Horse who traditionally has been closest to his master—as a working partner, as a playmate, and above all as a friend.

This tradition can be traced back for ages through much of the Quarter Horse's ancestry: First there were his remote forebears in Asia Minor, the horses that for centuries roamed the rocky deserts with the nomadic tribesmen. When their masters were thirsty, the mares gave them milk; when their masters slept at night, the horses hovered over them, ever alert to whicker at approaching danger. This was the blood that the Moors brought to Spain, where it was further refined and then brought to American shores in the vessels of the conquistadores. In the New World it played such a vital role that Bernal Díaz, the celebrated chronicler of the conquest of Mexico, was moved to exclaim: "After God, it was the horses!"

The horses that the Indians stole from the Spanish added a new dimension to their arts of war and hunting. And for the lonely cowpoke on the trail, in the early days of the American West, his Spanish-descended cow pony was often for days on end his sole source of companionship. For while it may be true that the modern Quarter Horse derives much of his speed and fire from his later "blooded" British ancestors, his basic traits of great kindness and adaptability are inherited from countless generations of "togetherness" with human beings.

* * *

Physically, the good Quarter Horse is one of the most pleasing of horses to look upon. His well-shaped, "breedy" head, with its small, dainty ears, wide-set eyes, and neatly squared-off muzzle, reflect his strong eastern background. His full neck is lightly arched at the crest and is in good proportion to the rest of his body. The shoulder slopes sharply; the chest is unusually deep and broad.

The Quarter Horse's forelegs are characterized by quite short cannon bones and medium-length pasterns. His short-coupled back, commencing in medium-high but quite sharp withers which run well back, is well-formed to accept the saddle. Perhaps his most distinguishing characteristic is the exceptional powerful musculature

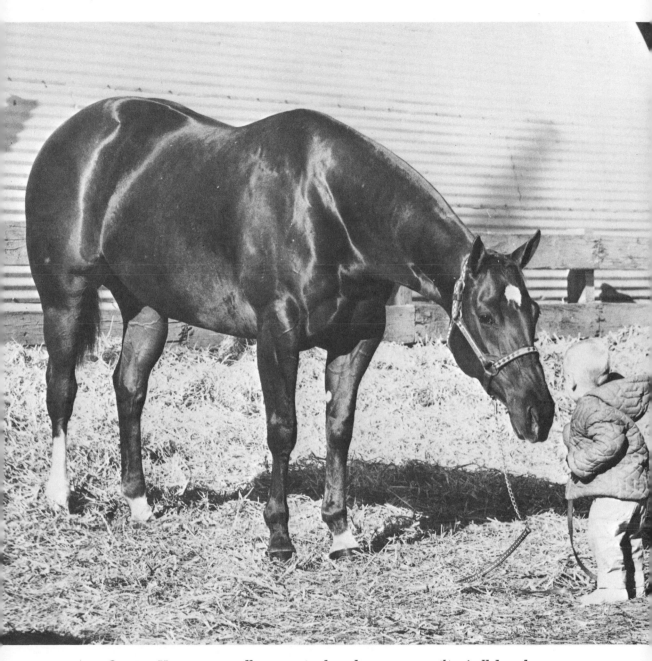

Quarter Horses, generally recognized as the most versatile of all breeds, are also the most companionable.

of his hindquarters, which rise through the loin to a point where, in extreme examples, he gives the illusion of being taller at the rump end than he is at the withers. Then he slopes off to a well-set tail. His bones are flat and clean but show much more substance than those of his more fragile cousins on the Thoroughbred side of his family.

His truly remarkable balance, both when standing still and when in motion, account for his fantastic ability to dart off in any direction, spin around and stop on a dime, without losing a jot of his poise. His extreme alertness, coupled with his unusually placid temperament, are responsible for that oft-quoted description of the Quarter Horse as a "sleepy little critter that can unwind like lightnin'." Not only can he do that, but, owing to generations of toughening on the arid western prairies, he can do it time after time without working up the smallest streak of sweat, when virtually any other horse would be lathered from head to tail.

In an article written for the American Quarter Horse Association's initial stud book, Robert J. Kleberg, master of the famed King Ranch at Kingsville, Texas, and a leading breeder of Quarter Horses and Thoroughbreds, stated: "If the range livestock men of America were asked to select the horse that is most useful for their purpose and that has contributed the most pleasure and satisfaction to their lives, I believe they would select the Quarter Horse, or the cross of the Quarter Horse on the Thoroughbred that has retained the Quarter Horse conformation. If asked to give their reasons for this choice they would say, 'Our horses have to live on the range and rely on the native shrubs and grasses for their food. The Quarter Horse takes on and carries enough flesh and muscle to stand the hard work that is required of him. He has a good, quiet disposition, is easy to gentle and train, has extreme early speed and the strength and sure-footedness to carry heavy weight over any kind of country. He stops and turns easily and does not become leg weary even when asked to stop and start quickly many times in the course of the day's roping, cutting or other work.' "

Apart from his great superiority as a stock horse, the Quarter Horse can do a number of other things. Some Quarter Horses can jump extremely well. (One of them, a registered Quarter Horse named Fire One, has represented this country on the United States Equestrian Team, as an open jumper.) But his ability to jump, as well as his blinding speed, are qualities that he inherits from the Thoroughbred side of his breeding chart. Generally speaking, how

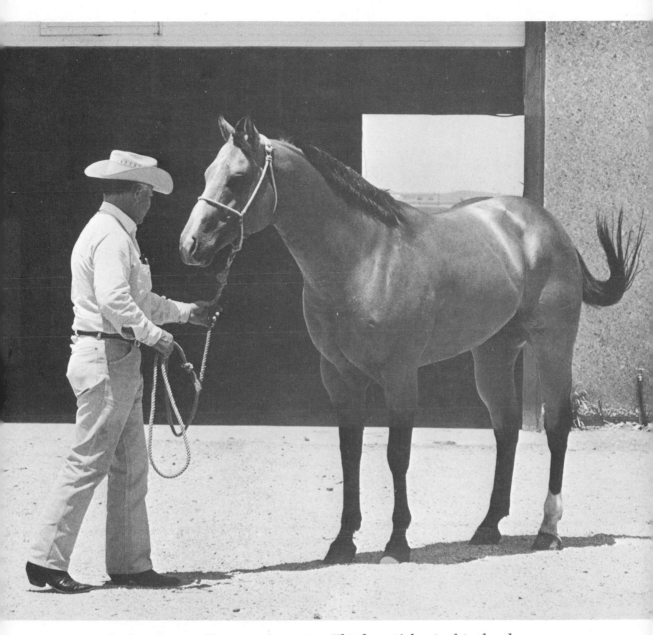

Perfect Quarter Horse conformation. This beautiful animal is the champion cutting horse Shu Twist, held by his owner, Mr. Rex Cauble, of Denton, Texas.

Perfect Thoroughbred conformation. This is the great French champion Sea Bird, now at stud at Darby Dan Farm, Lexington, Kentucky. Compare with the Quarter Horse on page 15.

fast he can run and how well he can jump will depend not only on how much but also on what kind of Thoroughbreds are in his background.

This statement is well-supported throughout the ups and downs of his breeding history. From the time that the Famous American Quarter Running Horses were burning up the race paths of colonial Virginia and Maryland, to the present day, it has held true that the fastest Quarter Horses have always been derived from a Thoroughbred stallion who passes on tremendous early speed (or "foot") when crossed to a "Quarter type" mare.

It became quite apparent, particularly in the several decades following the Civil War, that when the Quarter Horse became further removed from this kind of blood he temporarily lost some of this speed. Indeed, for a while it became a practice of race track "sharpies" in the west occasionally to pass off a "speedball" type Thoroughbred as a Quarter Horse for the purpose of winning money on bets. So successful were some of these swindles that the "ringer" had to live out his days under his false Quarter Horse identity for fear of the unpleasant consequences that might befall his owner should the secret leak out.

(That our pioneer forbears took their racing seriously is shown in a letter from a nineteenth-century British visitor to Houston, who wrote: "It is reckoned unsafe to attend the races there, indeed to reside in the Town a week after them, so desperate is the Bowie-knifing & pistolling on these merry making occasions.")

The later crossings back to Thoroughbred speed sires has restored the quality of great early foot to modern Quarter Horses—particularly to those of the racing stripe—and today they are probably closer in blood type to the colonial quarter pather than they were 50 years ago.

Certainly no one would dispute the statement that for any distance up to four hundred yards the racing Quarter Horse can beat any other breed. At 440 yards, the rangier, longer-striding Thoroughbred, if he is a particularly fast breaker, starts to catch up. In fact, the Thoroughbred record for the quarter-mile, set by Big Racket, in 1945, is $20\frac{4}{5}$ seconds, fractionally faster than the Quarter Horse mark of $21\frac{1}{2}$ seconds established in 1965 by Joe Sherry. Of course, this comparison is hardly fair since Quarter Horses are clocked from a standing start while Thoroughbred times are started when they activate an electric eye circuit some distance beyond the starting gate. However, it indicates some equality at this distance.

At any distance up to 400 yards, the Quarter Horse can beat any other breed. As he scrambles down the straightaway, the Quarter Horse (above) seems to grab at the ground. The longer-striding Thoroughbred (below) seems to become slightly air-borne, disdainful of the ground he covers so effortlessly.

And there have been a few Thoroughbreds of exceptional early speed which could run the quarter-mile against the best of Quarter Horses.

One such was Fred W. Hooper's Olympia, who defeated the Quarter Horse Champion Stella Moore in a special match race held in 1956 in Florida. (Stella Moore did have her excuses. Some say that she broke badly and seemed to waver and lose speed when she struck a soft spot in the "off" going. But as the man in the window says, "We don't pay off on excuses.") But generally speaking, the Thoroughbred that could match strides with a Quarter Horse even at 440 yards would have to be considered a genuine "freak."

The over-all superiority of the Quarter Horse up to the quarter-mile and the dominance of the Thoroughbred at greater distances than that is often erroneously explained by the statement that the Thoroughbred has more "stamina." This is a grave misapplication of the word. For example, when it comes to working all day under a blazing sun or in the teeth of a winter wind, carrying a heavy rider and his big stock saddle, the "stamina" of even the most ordinary Quarter Horse is such that he would outlast by hours the gamest Thoroughbred ever foaled.

The differences in their racing performances is explained by certain other dissimilarities between the two breeds of both a mental and a physical nature.

There is, for example, no question that the Quarter Horse's superior mental alertness and quick way of responding accounts for a good part of his success as a short race horse. This helps him to break fast. A number of Thoroughbreds with immensely successful racing records have been notably poor post horses, relying on plenty of time and track to overcome an early deficit with a strong finishing kick. But in a race which may be run off in fifteen or twenty seconds, there is not a foot of track that can be thrown away to humor the whim of the horse.

Instead, Quarter Horse trainers school their racers in such a way as to take the fullest advantage of their animals' naturally sharp reflexes, and it is maintained by many experts that many Quarter Horse events are won the instant the gate opens. When breeders of Quarter racing horses are shopping in the Thoroughbred market place for "improvement" stallions, the kind of sire they are looking for is the one whose charts show that he consistently broke on top and ran well on the lead. The gallant "come-from-behinder" has no appeal for them at all.

Then there are anatomical differences that account also in part for the Quarter Horse's blinding speed on the short course and the Thoroughbred's ability to go a route of two miles or more with comparative ease.

When the Quarter Horse jumps out for a start, propelled by his unusually powerful hindquarter muscles, his strong forelegs literally grab at the ground. Compared with the free-striding Thoroughbred, he seems almost to scramble down the straightaway. The horizontal plane through which he travels is more parallel to the ground than that of the Thoroughbred, and his shorter, quicker stride can be compared to the action of an automobile in low gear.

The Thoroughbred, whose muscles are, by comparison, longer and flatter, cannot gather himself so rapidly at the outset, but like a car in high gear, he runs effortlessly once he is rolling. He secures considerably less advantage from his longer, slimmer forelegs, and virtually his entire power plant is brought to bear on what racing people know as his "drive shaft," the exceptional length between his point of hip and point of hock. He runs through a horizontal plane which tilts upward at the forward end with the result that, as he gathers momentum, he becomes slightly "airborne."

Often too, the average Thoroughbred, though he may be taller and rangier than the typical Quarter Horse, is lighter in weight. The simple fact that he is toting less weight on his frame is another factor that partly explains his greater staying power.

❋   ❋   ❋

Dr. George Gaylord Simpson, professor of paleontology at Harvard University and horse historian *par excellance,* once made the observation that the horse was ideally suited to the needs of man because "he is both intelligent enough and stupid enough to do what we demand of him." Very true. But it must be borne in mind that the various requirements man has made of his historic partner have varied greatly in complexity, from the relatively simple-minded task of pulling a wagon or plow to the highly sophisticated maneuvers of "high school" dressage.

Even in the case of dressage, however, the trainer relies mainly on the horse's memory (which is excellent) to do something which

Quarter Horses (above) and Thoroughbreds (below) in full stride. Note the greater extension of Thoroughbred number 10 over the number 7 Quarter Horse.

he has previously been taught. In the case of the Quarter Horse used as a stock animal, the demand is even more intellectual since, in cutting cattle, he is actually called upon to think for himself, to improvise and employ his own initiative in coping with situations that are never the same twice.

His ability to do this results from the breed's so-called "cowsavvy," a quality which the Quarter Horse possesses to a degree far greater than any other horse. This is a trait which must be developed by skillful training. But it is, nevertheless, a basic part of the Quarter Horse's character that has been built into him by selective breeding which, astonishing though it may seem, can be traced back in history for 25 centuries or more.

This peculiar canniness in handling livestock comes, unquestionably, from the Spanish-descended horses which were found by the English colonists in the east and by the frontiersmen in the western plains. "Cow sense" was not a quality which suddenly emerged on the stock farms and ranches of the New World. It was in these horses then, and had been there for many centuries before they were shipped to the New World in the ships of the Spanish conquistadores.

From the naturalists' point of view, "cow sense" probably has its basis in the so-called "herding instinct" common to all members of the equine family of animals. It is certainly a fact that, of all living creatures, the horse is one of the most gregarious in his associations with other animal species. The first American pioneers going west reported seeing the wild descendants of the Spanish horses not only roving in great mustang bands of their own kind but also frequently running happily with herds of buffalo, antelope, and wild cattle.

The horse's recognition of, and generally amiable attitude toward, other animals is therefore, fundamentally, the reason why he can be trained to work with other kinds of livestock. But the Quarter Horse's truly extraordinary instinct for this kind of work is another matter again.

Historians have speculated that one of man's earliest uses of the domesticated horse was in the herding of other animals. The naturalist Pers Crowell points out that the dawn of the Age of Cultivation coincides approximately with the time that man stopped eating horse flesh, and he cites this as a reasonable "indication that horses were being used to help with the herds."

In his *Cavalcade of American Horses,* Crowell reconstructs the picture in these words: "We can well imagine, in the early domestication of animals, the happy thought one day striking a man that he could herd a band of wild cattle into a box canyon and hold it there until such time as he needed the meat more urgently. No doubt he brought food to these animals to sustain them while in live storage. From this beginning he possibly realized that it would be easier to herd them from one grazing area to another than to feed them himself."

While conceding that this is at best "educated guessing," Crowell goes on to construct his theory that nomadic peoples of very early times "eventually learned to use the horse as a mount to assist them in driving their flocks and herds from upland pastures to lower winter quarters."

It is, of course, anybody's guess at what point in ancient times man began to develop horses that were particularly adept at this sort of work. But it was evidently a practice of long standing when Greek traders brought the first fine horses of the nomadic tribesmen from Asia Minor into Europe.

The center of the horse-breeding industry in Greece was in the state of Thessaly. Less rugged in terrain than most of the Hellenic Peninsula, Thessaly was a sort of counterpart of our Kentucky "blue grass" region. Here, the Thessalonian horsemasters took the imported eastern horses and bred them to even greater refinement. Not only were the Thessalonians great breeders, but they were superior horsemen as well. Unlike the other Greek states which, because they were mountainous, depended for defense largely upon foot troops, the Thessalonian armed forces were centered around cavalry. (In due time, the horses and horsemen of Thessaly would play a vital role in the victories of Alexander the Great.) Similarly, their sports tended to the equestrian in character, as opposed to the track and field events so popular in other Greek states.

Veteran rodeo fans who believe that bull-dogging was born when old Bill Pickett in a fit of temper at a stubborn steer pitched himself on its horns and wrestled it to the ground, may be surprised to learn that precisely the same sport was practiced by the Thessalonian cowboys in the fifth century B.C. The historian Pliny describes in detail how the mounted Thessalonians ran down wild bulls, leaped on their heads, and flipped them to the ground by the horns. Knowing the great skill of the ancient breeders at developing horses for specific uses, we have every reason to believe that they might have created a strain of animals especially adept as "dogging" horses.

Not only did bull-dogging thrive in Greece, it spread out into Asia

ΤΑΥΡΟΚΑΘΑΨΙΩΝ ΗΜΕΡΑ

*Marble relief found at Smyrna representing horsemen pursuing bulls.
A similar relief has been found in excavations at Sardis.*

Minor. In such centers as Smyrna and Sardis, the ancient capital of
Lydia, it became enormously popular.

The Greeks, and later the Romans, were responsible for the wide
distribution of the eastern-type horses to the far reaches of their
empires. But ultimately it was Spain which became, in the words of
John Hervey, "the breeding ground of Europe's finest and most
valuable types of horses—due wholly to its constant infusions of
Oriental blood which reached all the way across North Africa and
back to Arabia, itself, where now all that was best and purest of
the entire classical breed of Asia Minor had found its final home
and refuge."

These infusions are thought to have come about first through
Phoenician traders who brought some eastern horses into the
Spanish peninsula. Hannibal's Carthaginian forces also passed that
way enroute to their ultimate defeat at the hands of the Romans
and deposited a number of additional blooded stallions. Finally, the
superbly mounted Moors, who were to dominate Spain for nearly
eight centuries, arrived. The stud which they established at Córdoba, based on four foundation stallions of the purest desert blood
and later to be the source of many of the horses the Spanish sent
to the Americas, probably had no equal as a breeding center.

It has often been pointed out that the Spanish conquistadores
who came to the New World were highly experienced stockmen
and that many of the horses they brought with them had been
specially bred for handling livestock. However, there is another
factor underlying inbred "cow sense" in our modern stock horses
that has been rather generally overlooked.

The Moors, when they established control over Spain, became great enthusiasts of the old Spanish sport of bullfighting, a pursuit which they not only took up themselves but also greatly refined. As anyone who has ever seen a bullfight can bear witness to, the fighting bull strains of Spain and Portugal bear little if any resemblance to the placid beef and dairy animals we are accustomed to seeing. They were—and are—extremely fast and shifty of foot, and dangerously aggressive by nature. Even before the time of Hannibal, the old Celtic inhabitants of Spain hunted these wild beasts as a sport. So fierce were these bulls that they were often imported to Rome and used in the same manner as lions were in spectacles in which criminals and religious dissenters were tossed into the ring to be gored to death.

In Moorish-ruled Spain, bullfighting became a diversion of the nobility. The fights were conducted entirely from horseback. It was not until 1700, long after the Moors had been driven from Spain, that the dismounted bullfighter, with his cape and sword, began to replace the mounted matador and his lance. These horses were sometimes of pure eastern ancestry and sometimes of the Andalusan breed which contained a touch of the native cold blood. Whole families of such horses with acutely sharpened stock sense were developed for the purpose of fighting bulls. Some of the strains have been preserved in Spain to this day, and on rare occasions a bullfight will be enlivened by the presence of a *rejoneador,* or mounted torero. In neighboring Portugal, the sport of fighting the bull from horseback is still very much in style.

Writing recently in *The Chronicle of the Horse,* Kathleen B. Velardi described the modern Spanish bullfighting horses: "They are not quite Arabian but have the short back, high arched tail and tiny hooves of the true Arab. They have the long legs and desirable breeding characteristics of the Thoroughbred, combined with the stockiness and stamina of a Morgan, and the strong shoulders and agility of a Quarter Horse. They have been bred to do their work." This horse, she said, shows "no more fear at the charge of a 1500 pound bull than he might from the charge of a playful yearling calf.

"Anyone," the writer adds, "who has any interest in watching cutting horses will thrill to watch these horses judge the speed of the bull's charge and carry their riders into range for the thrust." The forbears of these horses, she comments, were the horses of the Spanish conquistadores.

In another article, which appeared in the May 1966 issue of *The Western Horseman,* Dr. J. L. Korbacker tells of his visit to the ranch of the celebrated Portugese bullfighter and horse breeder, Joao Nuncio. This is his description of the animals bred and trained by Nuncio for bullfighting:

"It was quite evident that these were Andalusan horses, or the Portuguese or Peninsula horses, as they are known in Portugal. . . . The horses themselves are outstanding individuals, about medium in size, with well-set heads and necks so that they seem to collect absolutely naturally. They are very efficient; and more than this, they present a composite of elegance, of catlike quick movements, of instant responsiveness."

Dr. Korbacker's description of Nuncio's bullfighting mounts sounds as though he might have been describing a top cutting Quarter Horse.

The similarity in horsemanship used when riding a bullfighting and a cutting horse was demonstrated not long ago when a group of cutting horse people invited a Portuguese bullfighter, who had just given an exhibition of his art at a local arena, to try his hand at their sport. Riding a good Texas cutting horse, the maestro went at it as though he had been cutting cattle all his life.

Extensive selective breeding to sharpen their horses' stock sense was carried on for eight hundred years by the Moors and by the Spanish, and there cannot be any doubt that the quick reflexes and great agility of the modern Quarter Horse traces, in good part, to their bullfighting ancestors in the "old country."

Shortly after Columbus discovered the New World, and the Moors were finally expelled from Spain, the quality of the horses bred in Spain went into a gradual decline. While that nation continued for a few centuries longer in its role as a supplier of fine horses to the rest of Europe—notably to England, as we shall presently see— it was in Spain's American possessions that the best Spanish horses were being bred.

As early as 1493, on his second voyage to the Western Hemisphere, Columbus brought good seed stock to the colony at Santo Domingo. From here, breeding spread to other of the West Indian islands, notably to Cuba, from which came most of the horses used in the initial expeditions to the continental Americas. The horses bred in the Cuban royal stud were said to have been of the famous breed of Córdoba originally established by the Moors. Soon, in the

Bullfighting on horseback in Portugal. (Photo "Sni-Yan")

view of foreign visitors to New Spain, better horses were to be seen here than in the Spanish homeland.

The late J. Frank Dobie and other authorities have expressed the view that North America, particularly the silver-wealthy Viceroyalty of Mexico, received a generally better quality of horses than did South America. In *The Mustangs*, Dobie wrote: "One of the first acts of any successful Spanish general was to establish a hacienda for raising livestock. . . . Cortes, Alvarado and other conquistadores were raising horses before the Indians of Southern Mexico quit resisting."

In other, farther flung attempts at colonization, like that of Juan de Oñate, at Santa Fe, the Spanish never did succeed in wholly subduing the Indians, and the more deeply they penetrated into the continent the more their efforts to subjugate the red man were frustrated. By now, the Indians had long since shed their fear of the strange, prancing steeds and the noisy, but rather ineffective, firearms of the invaders. They were acquiring horses of their own at an ever-increasing rate, sometimes by illegal barter with the Spanish settlers but usually by wholesale thefts. Indeed, it was the boast of those great Indian horsemen, the Comanches, that the only reason they tolerated Spanish colonists in their territory was so that they could breed horses for their warriors to steal.

Just as the "cow sense" of the good horses he brought from Spain served the Spanish ranchero well in handling the great longhorn herds of his hacienda, so did this same quality benefit the Indian in his primary occupation, which was hunting.

Before he acquired the horse, the Indian had to pursue his favorite food, buffalo, on foot. This required much skill and endless patience and often resulted in slim pickings for the tribe; so slim, in fact, that they were often compelled to settle for less tasty fare. In lean times, it was not uncommon for the Indians to slaughter and eat some of the dogs which, early explorers tell us, abounded around every encampment and, until the coming of the horse, were the Indians' principal beasts of burden.

The horse greatly simplified the hunting of buffalo. The mounted buffalo hunters became the most important men in the western tribes. To them were assigned the swiftest and bravest horses. To quote Dobie again: "A horse had to be fast overtaking stampeding buffaloes. He had to be alert and quick in turning. With reins dropped on his neck, he came up on the right side to within fifteen or twenty feet of the buffalo selected by his rider. If the rider missed a shot and had to reload, an operation requiring two hands, the trained horse kept on after the same buffalo."

In a footnote, elsewhere in *The Mustangs*, Dobie makes the comment: "Trained by Indians, Spanish horses showed as much buffalo sense as, under vaqueros and cowboys, they showed cow sense."

It might be added that "buffalo sense," "fighting bull sense," and "cow sense"—the basic instinct to react to livestock for which the Moors and Spaniards had been selectively breeding for endless generations—are one and the same quality. And perhaps it is not too far-fetched to trace this characteristic all the way back to those ancient bull-doggers of Asia Minor, since, as we have seen, it was from here that the Moors brought the stock with which they equipped their Spanish stud farms.

In any event, it was to such tough, cow-, bull-, and buffalo-wise stock that our forebears blended in the swiftness of the English blood horse to create that rare combination of speed, agility and "cow savvy' that we find in the Quarter Horse of today.

The Quarter Horse inherited his "cow sense" from his Spanish forebears. (The Quarter Horse Journal)

The Quarter Horse can outthink the cow, actually anticipating his every move. This is the top cutting horse Chickasha Dan, Buster Welch up. Note that no bridle is used, and Buster sits with hands folded on the saddle horn.

The Thoroughbred Heritage

In the year 1764, a foal was dropped in England which would shortly have an effect so profound that it would reshape the entire course of light horse breeding. Prophetically, this horse was named "Eclipse," for indeed he eclipsed everything seen to that date on the English race courses.

Eclipse was the great, great grandson of an oriental sire purchased some six decades earlier, in Syria, by an English breeder named Thomas Darley. Two earlier stallions—Matchem, the grandson of the Godolphin Arabian (or Barb), foaled in 1748, and Herod, the great grandson of the Byerly Turk, foaled in 1758—were selected to join Eclipse as the three Thoroughbred "founding fathers." Even so, it was the overpowering race record and breeding prepotency (ability to pass on his best qualities to his offspring) of this mighty chestnut stallion that led British breeders to the conclusion that the finest seed of the blood horse should be conserved, perpetuated, and improved through a controlled breeding system. This resulted, in 1791, in Weatherby's General Stud Book and the establishment of the Thoroughbred family.

To racing, the Thoroughbred is a comparative newcomer. Even in America, the sport had long been popular before the Thoroughbred made his official bow. Nearly a century and a half earlier, Richard Nicholls, the British governor of New York, had laid out the first formal racing oval in this land on Salisbury Plain, Long Island, near the site of modern Belmont Park. And quarter racing, so popular among earlier Maryland and Virginia settlers, had already commenced its retreat from the fashionable Tidewater area.

In England, racing had been going on for so long that it is impossible to set even an approximate date for its origin, though it is believed to have been started by the Romans. We know that it was popular even before the coming of William the Conqueror. Actual turf records extend back as far as Henry II in the Twelfth

Century, and, except for the brief interlude of Cromwell and the Puritan Roundheads, it has been flourishing there ever since.

But because of the importance of the Thoroughbred in the formation of the Quarter Horse family, his background deserves to be studied.

It is not likely we shall ever know precisely what combination of blood types produced the Thoroughbred horse. With solemn conviction, scholars of the horse world such as Lady Wentworth have maintained that he is the product of the mating of outstanding oriental sires to mares which were themselves of pure Eastern descent. Lady Wentworth states flatly that the so-called "Royal Mares" of Charles II, which were supposed to have been the taproots of the Thoroughbred family, were without exception all obtained in the Eastern Mediterranean lands by agents of the crown. And, to this day, in some quarters, it still amounts to sacrilege even to suggest that the Thoroughbred horse is anything but a pure son of the desert.

But the evidence, both physical and historical, is much to the contrary. In many points of anatomy and performance characteristics, the Thoroughbred horse differs very markedly from the animal we know as an Arabian. The Thoroughbred is tall, long-legged and rangy with prominent withers. His head, while handsome in proportion to his body, lacks the refinement found in the best Arabian types. The Arabian is small, much less leggy, and much more compact. The withers are far less prominent, to the extent that in some examples he may give the illusion of being higher in the hind end than in the front, like the Quarter Horse. (As a matter of fact, a great many well-bred Quarter Horses resemble Arabians more closely than do Thoroughbreds—a fact which is undoubtedly due to the heavy oriental background on the Spanish side of their family.) In performance, the Arabian, though possessed of endless endurance, is among the least fleet of the light horse breeds while, of course, the Thoroughbred can defeat any make of horse at distances upwards of the quarter-mile.

The scientific evidence shows clearly that the horse is an animal of very slow evolution. (It took him some sixty million years to reach his present evolutionary stage, a process that man accomplished in something like one-sixth that time.) There have been no significant anatomical changes in the general horse types in the past million years. It is therefore impossible that in the few generations that separate the foundation sires of the Thoroughbred family from their supposedly all-eastern forbears they could have undergone such drastic anatomical changes as adding an extra vertabra to their spines and a hand (4 inches) or so to their stature without some outside breeding influence.

As the American writer John Wallace observed: "The increase in size cannot be accounted for on any other grounds than the introduction of the blood of some larger breed." But it is difficult to specify what that "larger breed" was. Indeed, the chances are that there was more than just one such strain involved.

But before going into that, let us for a moment consider the possibility that there were important differences between the various types of eastern horses themselves that contributed blood to the Thoroughbred. The old English, and even the early American, stud records are filled with references to "Arabians," "Barbs," and "Spanish Barbs." Unhappily for the historian, horsemen of earlier times were quite careless about how they applied these terms. It was often the case, for example, that a horse would be designated a "Barb' if he happened to be acquired on the Barbary coast. But he might well have been bred elsewhere because, as we have seen, there was heavy traffic in horses extending from Asia Minor, across North Africa, and, during the Moorish rule, into the Spanish penin-sula. This carelessness in the use of terms has led to the notion that all of these animals were more or less alike, with perhaps a shade more refinement being attributed to those bred in Asia Minor. But was this really the case?

We know, for example, that William Cavendish, the Duke of Newcastle, who is regarded as the greatest horseman of the seven-teenth century, placed Barbs at the top of his list in preference for blood, but had a poor opinion of Arabians, or at least of what he knew of them. Wrote the Duke: "I never saw but one of those horses, which Mr. John Markham, a merchant, brought over and said he was a right Arabian. Mr. Markham sold him to King James for 500 pounds, and being trained up for a course, when he run every horse beat him."

The description furnished by Richard Berenger, master of horse to the British crown as late as 1771, describes the Barb, which he says was then common in Western Europe, as having "withers standing high and fine." He describes it's gallop as "very rapid." Neither of these details fit the Arabian horse as we know it today.

Before we dismiss the notion that the modern Thoroughbred could possibly be of any but pure eastern blood, some consideration is due to the interesting theory offered by Mrs. Marguerite Farlee Bayliss, the author of the *Matriarchy of the American Turf*, a book which is used by every important Thoroughbred breeder in the United States. Writing in *The Thoroughbred Record* of March 27, 1926, Mrs. Bayliss advanced in some detail her belief that the modern Thoroughbred is indeed a true descendant of the desert Arabian, but of a breed which has long since vanished from Arabia. Recognizing the merits of what she calls "Arabs," the horses we know as such today, she nevertheless contends that the true Arabians "of the blood" were withdrawn long ago from the Arabian desert through heavy imports into England and elsewhere for use in creating the modern racing breed—the Thoroughbred.

While there isn't much evidence to support this theory, it may be true that the biggest and fastest stallions have been, over a long period of years, drained out of Asia Minor. (Throughout history, the Arabian tribespeople were more willing to part with stallions than with mares.) But, if so, this must have taken place a considerable time before the establishment of the Thoroughbred "founding fathers." For in no way does it explain how, for example, the little 15-hand Godolphin (some records say he was even smaller) could, in two generations, produce the 16.3-hand Matchem, a horse who by all accounts was very similar to the Thoroughbred of today—and a big one, at that.

Actually, England had been receiving periodic infusions of oriental blood since Roman times. Some historians claim that as early as Richard I's reign there were Arabian stallions standing in Yorkshire. But, unless we swallow whole Mrs. Bayliss' theory about the "different" breed of Arabian, we must look elsewhere for the explanations of the Thoroughbred's speed and size. And the most logical place to look is Spain.

Throughout the Dark Ages which followed the collapse of the Roman Empire, and prior to the invention of gunpowder, England and most of the rest of Europe depended, for military purposes, upon the so-called "great horses." These were the lumbering, cold-blooded giants—ancestors of the latter-day plow and draft horses—needed to carry the heavily armored knights into battle. The prime reason for England's importations and breeding of light horse types was for hunting and racing. Throughout this period, and for some time following, Spain was the principal supplier of such horses to most of the continent.

In that country, the breeding of fast light horse types dates all

The Thoroughbred, the athlete of the horse world, contributed qualities of body and character to the Quarter Horse. The Thoroughbred has many uses, but he is first and foremost a racing horse.

the way from the time of Hannibal, in the third century B.C., when, as noted in the previous chapter, that Carthaginian invader, in the course of his ill-fated expedition against Rome, brought many fine desert stallions into Spain. These were crossed on mares of the native, cold-blooded Vilana strain to produce a fine hardy breed that the Romans later exported to every part of their Empire. The Spanish light horse stock was further improved during the eight centuries of Moorish occupation, beginning in 711 A.D., as we noted in the preceding chapter, during which time many more eastern bloodlines were introduced into Spain and crossed on the good, part-blooded stock of that country to produce the Andalusan horse. Now, generally speaking, the laws of genetics tell us that when one type of horse is crossed upon another of like size, the resulting off-spring will be larger than either of its parents. So it was with the Andalusan. And there is little question that when we run across the term "Spanish Barb," or read of "Barbs acquired in Spain," the reference, in many cases, is to horses of the larger Andalusan variety —heavily eastern in background but not wholly "of the blood."

For nearly 500 years before the publication of the General Stud Book at the close of the eighteenth century, British sportsmen had a passion for Spanish horses. In 1327, in the year he ascended the throne, Edward III imported 19 Spanish "coursers" (race horses) and 50 "Andalusans." Henry VIII's agent, Roger Basing, was reported buying numerous mares and stallions in Spain. In James I's time, that Stuart monarch's friend, the Duke of Buckingham, developed what has been described as a "positive mania" for Spanish horses and, in 1623, acquired some 24 stallions in Spain for the king and 12 more for himself, together with many Andalusan mares and foals from the royal stud at Córdoba, that ancient Moorish breeding center.

From such stock, the English had evolved a fast race horse long before the coronation of Charles II, in 1660, when the so-called "father of the British turf" ushered in the modern age of racing. As early as 1606, that fine horseman, Gervase Markham, was moved to declare: "For swiftness what nation has brought forth a horse which excelled the English. When the best Barbaries that were ever in their prime, I saw them overcome by a black Hobbie, of Salisbury, and yet that black Hobbie was overcome by a horse called Valentine, which Valentine neither in hunting or running was ever equalled, yet was a plain English horse, both by syre and dam."

If we knew who that "plain English" horse's forbears were,

perhaps we could discover the mystery ancestor in the Thorough-bred family tree. But there appears every probability that not a few of them whinnied with a strong Spanish accent.

There is another breeding influence in the Thoroughbred back-ground which, although it cannot be measured with any precision, undoubtedly had some impact in the Thoroughbred's evolutionary stages before the appearance of the General Stud Book.

In England, hunting and racing have always been—and are today, for that matter—very closely related as the diversion of nobility. Many of the British monarchs, from the time of William the Conqueror to the present-day Queen Elizabeth, who were so instrumental in the formation of English racing stock, were also great devotees of the chase. And not infrequently, as in the case of the speedy "Valentine" described by Gervase Markham, horses that raced were also used as hunters.

It was, and still is, a common practice in breeding hunters to cross a blooded horse on a hefty draft mare—notably on the Per-cheron, a breed which itself has a strong flavoring of eastern blood in its background. The result of such a mating is a tall, rugged "hunter type" horse with a good bit of the blood horse's speed and stamina yet often better able to take the rough going of the hunting field than the more delicate Thoroughbred. Such breeding practices as this, before stud records came under the close scrutiny of the British Jockey Club in the early nineteenth century, may account for the sudden increase in height in the few generations between Eclipse, Matchem, and Herod and their admittedly "all eastern" forebears on the sire side.

While today we can only speculate how strong a part these various "impurities" may have played in the formation of early Thoroughbred blood stock, we can be certain that it is an over-simplification to say that the Thoroughbred emerged as a result of crossing eastern blood upon just any larger-sized strain. We can be equally sure that he is the result of a long series of breeding ex-periments involving a number of different strains that took place for many centuries before anyone ever thought of keeping a central stud record.

John Wallace is undoubtedly correct when he describes these practices. "The Anglo-Saxon race is fond of liberty," he wrote, with tongue well in cheek, and "every man exercised the liberty of mak-ing his pedigrees to suit himself. Thus, through advertisements, sales papers etc. great multitudes of fictitious pedigrees gained currency and were propagated from owner to owner, from generation to generation. On this point I speak from personal knowlege of a long lifetime in such affairs in my own country and I take it for granted that our English ancestors were no better or worse than we are ourselves. This was the condition of things in England . . . and when Mr. Weatherby was at work on the Stud Book he was overflowed with a flood of those bald-headed fictions, concocted by generations long past, and nobody could disprove them."

(That similar conditions were the rule in the early colonial southland in this country, where many American Thoroughbreds and Quarter Horses derived their breeding credentials, is admitted by no less an authority than Fairfax Harrison when he states flatly, in "The Background of the American Stud Book," that many of these pedigrees were "palpably constructed.")

But whatever went on "behind the barn" either in England or here, the end product—the Thoroughbred horse—whose true and accurately documented development has taken place only in the past century and a half, certainly justifies whatever means were employed to bring it about. Among all horses—probably among all animals which have been reared by man—he is the supreme example of selective breeding to attain a desired goal; in this case, not only speed and superb physique, but an inborn competetive spirit, a will to win, that make him the greatest athlete among all members of the equine clan. These qualities of body and character he has contributed to many other breeds, but to none in more generous measure than to his Quarter Horse cousin.

The Quarter Pathers

The fate that befell the first seven horses which the London Company sent to its pioneer settlement in Jamestown, Virginia, in 1610, was not a happy one. They were eaten.

At that, however, they may well have proved themselves indispensable, because the handful of colonists nearly starved to death during the bitter winter that followed their arrival.

Equine reinforcements were not long in following as the colony took permanent roots. In 1620, a shipment of 20 mares was recorded, and thereafter importations became increasingly frequent. These first horses to come from England were of the common light riding stock known as the Elizabethan "high" horses—from all accounts they were "high" in stature rather than in blood—and of the type vaguely referred to as "stots," and "rounceys."

Many more, and much better, horses began arriving in Virginia after the Puritans overthrew and beheaded Charles I, in 1649. At this time, many of the "cavalier" followers of the luckless Stuart monarch migrated to the so-called "Tidewater" of Maryland and Virginia. To Virginia alone, during this period, came more than a thousand well-to-do political refugees, bringing with them numerous animals of good eastern pedigree.

From the export of tobacco—the "brown gold" first brought to England by Sir Walter Raleigh—the colony soon became rich. The unpopular rule of the Puritans, in England, lasted but 11 years, but the cavaliers who had fled from it were, for the most part, doing so well that they had little desire to return. On the contrary, more settlers, attracted by the riches to be found in the New World, were streaming in, often bringing with them indentured servants who hoped to serve out their terms of bondship and strike out for themselves in the booming colonies. Here too came convicts whose terms had been commuted to colonial exile, and, in ever-increasing numbers, African slaves in the holds of the New England slave ships.

41

The society that sprang up in Virginia and Maryland, and shortly thereafter in the rich rice country of South Carolina, was feudal to the extent that it consisted almost wholly of "haves" and "have nots." And even among the "haves," a sharp distinction was made between the members of the blue-blooded cavalier aristocracy and the newly rich merchant class. (It was, for example, forbidden by law for a gentleman to make a wager with a commoner, under penalty of having to sit in the stocks.)

It was only natural that, as soon as possible, the colonial aristocracy should turn to the favorite English pastime of horse racing. The densely wooded countryside, however, prevented for some years the establishment of a formal race track such as the one which Governor Nicholls had implanted on the open meadows of Long Island. So the colonists revived a sport, said to have been devised by the ancient Saxons in England, called quarter pathing. This consisted of short, match races between two horses.

In producing horses suited to this form of racing, the settlers were not long in discovering that, by mating the blood stock they had brought from England to the "native" Chickasaw breed, they were able to come up with a horse of such exceptional speed over short distances that its like had not been seen before. A Mr. J.F.D. Smith, who traveled extensively in the colonies at the time, wrote of these horses: "I am confident that there is not a horse in England, nor perhaps in the whole world, that can excell them in rapid speed, and [they] likewise make an excellent saddle horse for the road."

Much has been written and much controversy still swirls about the origin of the Chickasaw strain of horses. It is a certainty that they were the wild descendants of horses brought over by the Spanish. But, beyond that simple fact, there lie some unsolved questions. For some time, a legend persisted that they were descended from horses which had somehow survived the ill-fated expedition of the conquistador Hernán de Soto in 1539 to what is now the southeastern part of the United States, or possibly an even earlier expedition to that part of the continent by Panfilo Narvaez. This theory has been thoroughly exploded. However, it does appear that the Indians made off with some horses that the Spanish had brought to Florida later on. Horses of such origin were referred to as Seminoles or Creeks. They were described as being quite small and "capricious" by disposition.

Another horse, also of Spanish origin, was somewhat larger and generally of better quality and temperament. These were the horses specifically referred to as Chickasaws, sometimes Chocktaws. Most authorities believe these animals came from Spanish outposts in Mexico and the American southwest, and had been passed eastward, from tribe to tribe, as the Indian acquisition of the horse spread across what are today our "deep South" states.

There was doubtless some interbreeding between the Seminole and Chickasaw types, at least to an extent that it is not easy now to separate them as to exact strain. In any event, the colonists found the better specimens of these horses to be such excellent mounts that they were busy acquiring them even before there were any substantial importations of blood horses from England.

In fact, the hunting of these so-called "wild" horses was itself a popular diversion of the colonial Virginians. Robert Beverly, who wrote extensively on sport in the colonies, describes how the mounted hunters, accompanied sometimes by dogs, pursued those animals which grazed "in the woods of the Uplands." They were, Beverly notes, "so swift that tis difficult to catch them; and when they are taken tis odds but their Grease is melted, or else being old they are so sullen that they can't be tam'd." Apparently the Indians were more skillful at catching these creatures, because it was from them that the colonists got most of their horses.

So extensively did the English colonists breed to these little Spanish-descended horses that, within a century, the average height of the individual horse had dwindled by a full hand and a half. But they were rewarded with a horse that was far better suited to their needs than those they had brought from England.

Not only were the cross-breds speedy and spirited, but they were also tough as rawhide. Their ancestors had lived for generations in a wild state or under the crude care of the Indians—not that they fared much better at the hands of the colonists. Several writers of the times took note of the shabby treatment the colonists gave to their ordinary saddle and work horses. Wrote the Frenchman Durand of Dauphine: "I do not believe there are better horses in the world, or worse treated. All the care they take of them at the end of a journey is to unsaddle, feed a little Indian corn and so, all covered with sweat, drive them into the woods, where they eat what they can find, even though it is freezing."

Visitors did note, however, that considerably better care was taken of the horses that were used for racing, though these too must have looked odd to persons accustomed to watching the sport in England. Not only were the speedy quarter pathers pint-sized but, due to the fact that they were never clipped and frequently were left out in the bitter cold, they were also often exceedingly shaggy.

Starting on the streets of the new settlements, quarter racing soon became the rage of the colonies. Though it was most popular in Tidewater Maryland and Virginia, there is evidence that it was by no means wholly confined to that area. That some form of short, road racing was practiced even in puritanical New England is evident from the legislation enacted in a number of communities forbidding it.

As early as 1674, Plymouth Colony provided for a fine of five shillings, or one hour in the stocks, for "any person who shall run a race with a horse . . . in any street or common road." Newport, Rhode Island, had similar laws on its books, as did Philadelphia, though in the latter city public safety rather that public morals seems to have been the reason. (Horse racing could hardly have offended William Penn, an ardent enthusiast of the turf and importer of some of the finest early blood stock.)

In New Jersey and New York, where there was less stringent supervision of public behavior, and where there were open fields in which horses could be raced without endangering the life and limb of the pedestrian, quarter racing was evidently quite popular. This was particularly true on Long Island, where it remained in vogue many years after end-to-end distance racing came to that part of the country. Sporting chronicles of the day make frequent reference to quarter matches held there.

As there would be later on between Thoroughbred owners of the North and South, there was a similar intersectional rivalry among Quarter Horse men. Writing in *The Spirit of the Times,* a Tennessee gentlemen was provoked to complain that "Long Islanders bray mightily on their Quarter nags."

It became a practice from time to time for the Southerners to smuggle one of their fleetest Quarter Horses into Long Island for the purpose of effecting a betting coup. Elaborate precautions were often taken to conceal the animal's true identity so that his backers could get a nice long price on their runner. Not infrequently, the stunt would be pulled off to the considerable profit of the smugglers. But on at least one notable occasion it failed to work for the sort of reason that plagues "sure thing" bettors to this day.

In this instance, a champion quarter pather was spirited into Long Island from Virginia, as half of a draft team. The animal

Early quarter racing was colorful if not completely honest. The caption for this engraving from "A Quarter Race in Kentucky" reads: "A rough-hewn fellow, who either was, or pretended to be, drunk, was bantering to run his mare against any horse that had ploughed as much that season."

helped pull a wagon around for long enough to lull any possible suspicions on the part of the betting fraternity. The conspirators were already counting up in their minds the bundle of Yankee dollars they expected to take home with them when they entered their innocent-looking cart horse in a race. However, when the event was run their "ringer" was soundly thrashed by a "Long Island flyer," and his backers instead of collecting money had to pay it out.

Popular though it appears to have been in other parts of the country, it was in the Tidewater South that for a good century quarter racing was truly an important part of what historians call the "Cavalier Culture." If we are to believe eyewitness accounts of those times, we must assume that the word "culture" must here be employed in its loosest possible sense. A French visitor to colonial Virginia noted that "horse-racing, cock-fighting, and boxing matches, are standing amusements for which they neglect all business."

In Jamestown, and later in Williamsburgh where the capital was relocated in 1676, the city fathers found it necessary for the safety of the citizenry to ban racing in the streets. Thereafter it was conducted on paths—usually two parallel strips—a quarter of a mile to five hundred yards in length, sometimes hacked out of the virgin forest but usually located in an unused field near a church, tavern, or other familiar landmark.

These straightaway racing strips were from 12 to 20 feet in width, with an open space at the start where the horses were jockeyed into position, and beyond the finishing post, where the judges (or "end men") were stationed, there was another open space for pulling up. Over the race path, the two horses were supposed to run on parallel courses without at any time crossing over into each other's path. In the beginning, the owners, "gentlemen all," usually rode their own horses. Something less than "gentlemanly," however, was the conduct of many of these events, in which the riders often used their whips and legs in trying to unseat their opponents. Fixing and "throwing" races also appears to have been a fairly common practice.

Racing wagers—tobacco and other negotiable items, as well as money, were frequently put up as stakes—were considered as legally binding contracts, and the outcome of many quarter races was determined in court rather than at the finish line. Not only did race results often wind up as lawsuits, they also quite frequently

This statue at Claremore, Oklahoma, memorializes the late Will Rogers. It is probably the only equestrian statue (horse and rider) in which a Quarter Horse was used as a model. (American Quarter Horse Association)

ended in free-for-alls. Indeed, brawling over horse races, cock-fights, and gambling in general, became so common that, in 1748, a statute had to be enacted forbidding such indignities on the persons of His Majesty's subjects as "eye-gouging, nosebiting, and the hacking off of limbs."

We can gather that such matters had gotten pretty far out of hand to bring about such legislation because the cavalier tradition was both lenient and lusty, and would remain so after the Revolution and up until the time of the Civil War. As often as not the governor and his party were active participants in such sports as hunting and racing, as later on were presidents Washington, Jefferson, and Jackson.

Such moral restrictions as existed were imposed by the very tolerant Church of England. Far from being opposed to racing, many of the clergy were ardent followers of the turf. The distinguished James Blair, colonial deputy of the Bishop of London, and founder of William and Mary College, was also the presiding officer of the Williamsburgh Jockey Club, an organization which claims the distinction of being the oldest such body in the country.

The so-called "sporting parsons," a common sight at English race meetings, were equally conspicuous at the quarter paths of the Tidewater. Generally speaking, these churchmen exerted a moderating influence. This was particularly true of Blair, whose oath as a priest was, on at least one known occasion, found to be acceptable evidence in court in deciding the outcome of a disputed race.

But there were some notable exceptions. One such was the Rev. Thomas Becket, whose excesses were such that he had to be relieved of his spiritual labors by the Royal Governor. Explaining this action to the Bishop of London, the governor wrote that "Mr. Becket is a man of strong constitution; loves drink perhaps too well, and living in the Northern Neck where drinking and boxing is too much in fashion has been tempted to quarrel; for being unpolished, he is bold and hardy in his temper, and has not yet learned to turn the other cheek."

No one seems able to fix an exact date for the first quarter race in the colonies. The earliest known path appears to have been located in Henrico County, not far from Richmond. Others were located in the "Northern Neck," a flat expanse between the Potomac and Rappahannock rivers. The sport spread quickly into the Eastern

Shore area of Virginia and Maryland, that part of those two states which is cut off by Chesapeake Bay.

Young Fire, owned by one John Gardiner, of Westmoreland, and a horse named Smoker, owned by a Mr. Joseph Humphries, are the most frequently mentioned quarter pathers in the era preceding the arrival of the great stallion Janus.

Quarter races were generally held on Saturday afternoons. From the journals and private papers of visitors to the Tidewater, we can reconstruct a lively picture of these meetings. We can almost see the dandified colonial gentlemen in their carriages accompanied by their ladies tricked out in their lavish Parisian finery; the seedy looking indentured servants, the grinning slaves and solemn Indians packed along both sides of the race path. Among them circulated peddlars and purse-snatchers, fortune-tellers and faith healers. Tents and wooden booths purveyed strong drink to the already worked-up throng of race-goers, so that by the time the race was off, the excitement of the crowd had reached fever pitch.

The horses were supposed to go from a standing start at the tap of a drum, the blast of a musket, or sound of a bugle. Usually, however, the riders had their animals circling, rearing and plunging at the starting line, each seeking to get a starting advantage over the other. Then they were off thundering down the straightaway to the screaming encouragement of the crowd. As they flashed, often neck and neck, past the finish post, there would be a hushed silence as the judges tried to decide on a winner, followed by a great outcry, blending the exultation of the winners with the disappointment of the losers, as the result was declared.

So hectic became the circumstances surrounding these and other public events, that as early as 1710 the General Assembly of Virginia had to intervene with a statute which prohibited "setting up booths, arbors, and stalls, at court houses, race fields, general musters and other public places, where . . . the looser sort of people resort, get drunk, and commit many irregularities." This law appears, from all accounts, to have been generally ignored, and despite the "irregularities," the race meets must have been great fun—at least for those who emerged unscathed.

John Bernard, a young actor who had traveled through those parts, later wrote that the quarter matches were the "most animated" sport he had ever encountered. In particular, he describes the delight of the onlookers, "hallooing, jumping and clapping their hands, more especially if the horses happened to jostle and one of the riders had been thrown off with a broken leg."

There was an essentially democratic flavor to colonial quarter racing which a Mrs. Anne Ritson, an Englishwoman married to a Norfolk merchant, captured in this quaint little verse:

> *A race is a Virginian's pleasure*
> *For which they always can find leisure;*
> *For that, they leave their farm and home,*
> *From ev'ry quarter they can come*
> *With gentle, simple, rich, and poor*
> *The race-ground soon is cover'd o'er*
> *Males, females, all, both black and white*
> *Together at this sport unite.*

Mrs. Ritson may have labored a bit with her rhyming, but she expresses rather neatly the sentiment of the unknown philosopher who observed: "All men are equal on and under the turf."

Mighty Janus

Quarter racing was in its late twilight in Tidewater Maryland and Virginia when the eighteenth century turned the midpoint, though it still flourished in "southside" Virginia and North Carolina. While New York remained—and would remain for some years to come—the only formal racing oval in the British New World colonies, some authorities believe that end-to-end "distance" racing in Virginia may have started as early as 1691 in this tobacco-rich part of the old Southland. It made its appearance in Maryland about the same time.

As in England, there was in the Tidewater a strong association between hunting and racing. The first hound pack to come to America was brought over by a well-to-do Maryland settler named Robert Brooke, the son of a member of Parliament, way back in 1650, and by the 1730's fox-hunting was a well-entrenched pastime of the upper class throughout this part of the country.

Hunting inevitably gave rise to the informal sort of steeplechasing known as point-to-point racing, over fences and natural obstacles such as brooks, which is popular to this day along the southeastern seaboard. The going was long and rugged—the modern Maryland Hunt Cup is run at four miles over 22 timber fence jumps—and required horses of extraordinary stamina, or "bottom."

Both hunting and steeplechasing undoubtedly promoted the interests of the "stayer" and worked to the disadvantage of the short-distance horse. There was now, moreover, more cleared land available for end-to-end racing. And while the Tidewater could not boast of a full-fledged race track such as the New Yorkers enjoyed, they made do as best they could.

A large open field would be selected with an infield staked out with tall poles outside of which the horses were required to run. Contemporary descriptions of these primitive race courses picture

The sport of steeplechasing, imported from England, gave impetus to the development of horses of greater endurance. Here is the modern version of the sport as practiced at Belmont Race Track in New York.

them as covering much uneven surface, rendered the more haz-
ardous by stumps, bumps, ruts, and the like, and by irregular, tricky
turns. The first actually recorded meeting of this sort was held in
Hanover County, Virginia, over a three-mile course, in 1737. From
this date on, the longer races became increasingly popular with
colonial sportsmen.

To bear his colors in the four-mile "heat" racing, which was in
vogue in the 1750's, Mr. Mordecai Booth, a prosperous planter and
ship-owner of Gloucester, Virginia, imported a smallish but very
well-bred stallion named Janus.

At this time, Janus was about ten years old—not an uncommonly
old age for racing in an era when horses did not start until they
were five. By most accounts, he stood little better than 14 hands,
was very solidly made, and of a color which we now call a bright
chestnut. Edward Skinner describes him as "from the shoulders
back . . . the most perfectly formed horse ever seen in Virginia, by
the most skillful connoisseurs; he was remarkable for roundness
of contour, strength of articulation . . . indicating great powers in
his whole conformation."

Until comparatively recent years, there was some controversy
over his breeding identity. But it has been established to the apparent satisfaction of all that he was the same horse who was known
in England by the names of "Stiff Dick," and "Little Janus," a son
of English Janus, by the Godolphin. His unnamed dam was by Fox,
whose grand-daughter was the celebrated Cub mare, often called
"Queen Mother of the American Turf."

In England, Little Janus had raced in the silks of Mr. Anthony
Langley Swymmer, a distinguished British sportsman and early
member of the Jockey Club. He had a superior racing record, winning impressively twice in four-mile heats, until a "foul sinew"
forced his retirement. He stood in Mr. Swymmer's Oxfordshire
stud from 1753 until 1755, at which time Mr. Swymmer sold him
to the prominent breeder, George Grisewood, of Litchfield, from
whom Booth acquired him shortly afterward. (There has always
been some uncertainty about the date of Janus' arrival in this
country. Some accounts have placed it as early as 1752. However,
the diligent John Hervey, historian of The Jockey Club, found
evidence in England to indicate this later date is the more reliable.)

In Virginia, Janus recovered his soundness and won again in
four-mile heats. He remained four years in the Old Dominion. Then,
unaccountably, he was dispatched on a long tour of stud duty in

"southside" Virginia and North Carolina. At this time, quarter racing, while declining rapidly in the Tidewater, had not wholly vanished from that region. It is probably a safe guess that Janus had already revealed himself to be a superior short-distance horse sire, and this was the reason for his exile to a part of the country where the sport was still popular.

In any event, he left a good reputation behind him in the Tidewater. To quote Skinner once more: "His stock partook of [his] qualities to an eminent degree, and for thirty or forty years they were considered as 'peculiar stock,' as they invariably exhibited even in the third and fourth generations from the old horse the same compactness of form, strength and power. The Janus stock have exceeded all others in the United States for speed, durability and general good form."

As a sire of quarter runners, Janus wasted little time in branding an imprint that would last for many generations thereafter. In May of 1832, when the recollections of his days were still green in the memories of old-timers, there appeared in the American Turf Register (Vol. 3) this account of "Quarter Racing of the Olden Time":

"For some years previous to the war of the Revolution, Quarter mile racing was the fashionable amusement in the State of North Carolina and the southern part of Virginia. Old Janus stood many years on the Roanoke, propagating a beautiful, hardy and speedy race of horses, and, as the gentlemen of fortune, in those days, were breeders of fine horses, they encouraged that type of racing to which their stock was best adapted."

This stock, of course, was the blend of Chickasaw with the early blood horse types that had already proved its mettle on the quarter paths of the Tidewater.

Apparently at the time to which the Turf Register's anonymous correspondent makes reference, quarter racing had all but ended in this part of the country too, for he concludes his account with a description of one of the last of these events, one which, since it involves a son of Janus, may be worth re-telling here.

This contest contained the elements of deceit and double-crossing that appear to have been just "part of the game" in those times, in distance matches and quarter races alike. For this reason, apparently, the writer chose to cloak the participants with anonymity.

Briefly, a Col. D——y, of Virginia, proposed to a Mr. J, of North Carolina, that since quarter racing was going out of style that they have one more race, "and for such a sum as both should remember." The stake agreed to was one hundred hogsheads (147,000 lbs) of Petersburg-inspected tobacco, the event to be run at even weights, each horse carrying 160 pounds.

Mr. J's entry was his prize short horse Paoli, "a swift son of Janus." When he arrived at the race paths on the appointed day, he was advised by his groom that Col D——y was not running a horse of his own, as stipulated in the wager, but had rung in a big, strong filly "evidently possessing great strength . . . and a high reputation, having never lost a race." This equine Amazon belonged to a gentleman identified as Col. A.

Since it was the practice of the time to give female quarter-runners a 12-yard handicap, this made Paoli's job all the more formidible. Indignantly, Mr. J sought out Col. A, who happened to be at the course, and bitterly scolded him for allowing his opponent the use of the filly in direct violation of an agreement he had made earlier with this same Col. A not to do so. Col. A replied that, unfortunately, he had suffered a lapse of memory when he made that deal and had overlooked a previous arrangement with Col. D——y, which permitted the latter to run the filly in any race of his choosing.

Though apparently he smelled a rat, Mr. J sportingly went ahead with the contest. Because of the size of the bet and the tension brought about by the foregoing circumstances, the race was run off in dead silence. "Not a man drew his breath—nothing was heard but the clattering of the horses. They passed with the noise and speed of a tempest."

The crowd remained tense and silent until, after much deliberation, the judges gave Col. D——y his come-uppance and announced that Paoli had won by 23 inches. Mr. J sold Paoli shortly thereafter for what was then the huge sum of five hundred dollars, but his reputation discouraged "all hope for using him as a racer in that part of the country."

Mr. J's Paoli was but one of the countless speedy animals which Janus produced in his day. Because of the sloppy records kept by many of the horsemen of that time, we shall never know just how many great quarter pathers the old boy actually did sire. But it is apparent that his blood mixed, or "nicked," so well with the good class of quarter mares to which he was bred that, although the Quarter Horse pattern was well established long before he made his appearance in the stud, his breeding influence thereafter almost

The world's richest horse race is the All-American Futurity—for Quarter Horses only—held at New Mexico's Ruidoso Downs. In 1967 the purse was roughly half a million dollars. (American Quarter Horse Association)

wholly dominates the formative period of the American Quarter Horse family.

He appears in the direct line of descendancy of nine of the 11 original families. Besides his own family, those established by his sons, Twigg and Babram, and by his grandson, Bacchus, all sprang from Janus mares as well. In P.N. Edgar's American Turf Register of 1833, there are listed over a hundred horses and mares of Janus descent, some to the fourth generation and many of straight line breeding, who are identified as F.A.Q.R.H. (Famous American Quarter Racing Horses). And though thinned and absorbed by the introduction of new blood, his presence can still be felt in modern Quarter Horse families, notably those of Peter McCue and Copperbottom.

In his fantastic prepotency, his ability to stamp his get with his own likeness, Janus has often been compared with that gallant little New Englander, Justin Morgan, who was to become the father of the entire tribe of horses that bear his name. But the fact that he was able to produce so many "self-portraits" during his long stay south of the Tidewater was in no small measure due to the kind of mares he covered. The late John L. O'Connor, revered as the "sage of Schuylerville," and one of America's most profound students of bloodlines, had this interesting observation to make:

"We know that horsekind was no novelty to the early emigrants who had to but catch or make trade with the Indians, the stock ranging the coastal territory from Florida northwards. This stock was not native original, but of Spanish origin and Spanish horses were for the most part Barbs. Now the Godolphin 'Arabian' was not an Arabian—he was a Barb. Janus was a grandson of the Godolphin. Janus 'nicked' well with the Chickasaw stock. Were these 'nicks' chance, or examples of 'like produces like'?"

Certainly the notion that Janus could run at distance but get nothing except short-distance horses—a still popular impression— is as false as it could be. As John Randolph wrote in Volume 1 of the American Turf Register: "Among the vulgar errors, perhaps the most absurd is that the stock of Old Janus wanted [lacked] bottom. This arose from his getting the speediest Quarter Horses out of ordinary mares. . . . Whenever he had blood mares, he got horses that ran any distance." The record bears this out.

While Janus was without question a veritable titan in the formation of the early Quarter Horse families, his impact on the American Thoroughbred stud book, which comes down on the female side, was not a bit less important. The "Matriarchy of the American Turf" contains nearly 14 pages devoted to "The Janus Mares" and their illustrious offspring. Indeed, as Mrs. Bayliss, the authoress comments, "Old Janus stands as Noah stood among the people of the Genesis." The most outstanding of his mare families is the Maria West clan from which was descended Regret, by Broomstick, the only filly ever to win the Kentucky Derby and one of the greatest of her sex ever to run in this country. Another descendant was the "galloping hatrack," Exterminator, by McGee, Willis Sharpe Kilmer's immortal old gelding who won 50 of a hundred starts (including the Derby) in an eight-year career that saw him unplaced only 16 times. Among these achievements was his winning of the Saratoga Cup at a mile and three quarters in four successive years and the Pimlico Cup, at two miles and a quarter, no less than three times. These feats would hardly indicate any "short" breeding in his background.

No matter how you look at it, a more remarkable sire than old Janus would be hard to find. When mated to speed he begat even more speed, and when crossed on bottom produced even greater bottom. He stands unique to this day in the stud books of the American Thoroughbred and Quarter Horse.

Horses in the New Nation

The War of the American Revolution produced no famous cavalry engagement. The still heavily forested countryside prevented any massive clashes of mounted men, a situation which worked to the advantage of the Americans. At this period in her history Britain had superb horse troops, which she was unable to bring to bear against His Majesty's rebelling subjects.

However, many horses were commandeered by both sides in the conflict to serve as officers' mounts, to draw artillery pieces, and to work in the baggage trains. The effect upon the still rather slender horse stock of the region was disastrous. During the war years racing was virtually halted everywhere save in New York, where it was continued in a rather limited way for the amusement of the large British force garrisoned in that city.

In Tidewater Virginia, quarter racing—except among a few die-hards—was extinct. (In Maryland it clung on a half century or so longer.) A good 20 or 30 years earlier it had been almost wholly displaced by distance racing of gruelling best-of-three four-mile heats. Therefore, for some time prior to the war, breeding activity in these parts was concentrated on producing horses of the "blood" type which in a few decades' time would be officially designated as "Thoroughbred." The quarter pather was still fairly well established in "southside" Virginia and in parts of the Carolinas, where the seed of Janus continued to make its mark on the turf. Here, as elsewhere, however, racing and breeding had been thrown into total confusion by the Revolution.

In his history of the South Carolina Jockey Club, Dr. John B. Irving ably describes the conditions that prevailed in that part of the country:

"The independence of the country having been declared, no event of interest occurred on the turf for many years. Not only were all the horses thrown out of training, but on the appearance of Lord

Intelligent, companionable, and versatile, Quarter Horses make excellent performing horses, such as these in the Barnum and Bailey Circus.

Cornwallis's army in the low country, they were either used as chargers by those who had taken up arms in the defense of the country, or they were hid in the swamps, adjoining the different plantations on which they were bred to prevent them from being carried off by the British."

Of the many horses that were concealed in the woods and swamplands of South Carolina, none was more celebrated than the stallion Flimnap, a sire which, like Janus, is of great importance to both the Quarter Horse and Thoroughbred families in America. Like Janus, Flimnap was a direct descendant of the Godolphin, being by South, a grandson of the Godolphin's, and out of a mare of the same breeding. Also like Janus, Flimnap, who was foaled in 1765, possessed the dual breeding characteristic of being able to transmit lightening speed to his offspring when crossed on mares of the Chickasaw type, and great staying power when mated to "blooded" brood mares.

So great was the reputation of this stallion, that it became an obsession of the British troops in Carolina to seize him at any cost. Flimnap's owner, Major Isaac Childs Harleston, who was then serving with the Continental troops commanded by General Nathanael Greene, was equally determined that this should not happen. Thanks to the devotion of his family and his servants, he won out though not without a succession of heroics that rival the finest efforts of Hollywood script writers.

At the time these events took place, Lord Cornwallis had established his headquarters at Silk Hope, a scant two miles from the Harleston Plantation where Flimnap and other animals in the Major's fine stud were quartered. The British were well aware of this and made numerous forays in an effort to capture him. Each time, however, friendly neighbors tipped off the plantation that the British were coming and the animals were led out into the seclusion of the swampy wilderness that surrounded the mansion.

Finally, the British did succeed in laying hands on one of the Major's stable boys. First they tempted the lad with offers of rich rewards if he would tell them were Flimnap and the others were concealed. When he refused to do so, they threatened to hang him and, when he continued to refuse to divulge the hiding place, strung him up to a tree and departed, fuming over their most recent frustration. After they left, another servant, who had remained in hiding, ran out and cut him down. A flicker of life still remained in the faithful groom and after much labor to save him he was finally revived to receive the grateful thanks of the Harleston family.

Flimnap, after this close call, was spirited off to a hiding place in North Carolina. But his adventures had not ended.

Some time after this attempt, things returned to normal in the vicinity of the Harleston Plantation and Flimnap was brought back. Somehow, the word leaked out to the British and again they became obsessed with the thought of capturing him. At this time, the British forces in the area were commanded by an intemperate Scot who, because of his vile temper and irrational acts, had earned the nickname of "Crazy" Campbell.

Campbell vowed he would take Flimnap and, upon hearing that the animal had been returned, he dispatched troops to raid the plantation. This time, however, they were intercepted by Continental forces and, in a brisk skirmish in which Major Harleston was a participant, they were put to flight.

Crazy Campbell was infuriated and set out himself at the head of a strong detachment to revenge his defeat by plundering and burning the plantation. On receiving the news that he was coming, the servants and field hands fled into the marshes, leaving the ladies of the establishment to shift for themselves.

Now it happened that one of these, a colonial belle of considerable wit and beauty, recalled that upon several occasions when she had been entertained in Charleston by relatives sympathetic to the British Crown, that Campbell had demonstrated a marked interest in getting better acquainted with her. Now, as the vengeful Scot and his band of looters drew near, she went out to greet him, smiling her most cordial greetings.

The British commander was totally taken aback, and bidding his soldiers to refrain from doing any damage to the plantation, he entered the house and enjoyed what Irving describes as a "long and a pleasant visit," eventually taking leave of the household "in the kindest and most friendly manner." Flimnap again was saved.

In the stud, Flimnap proved himself worthy of all the efforts that had been made on his behalf. While he established no official Quarter Horse family, Flimnap and another South Carolina stallion named Fallower, from whom the "modern" sire Steel Dust is said to trace his descent, were of paramount importance in this stage of the breed's development. Both Flimnap and Fallower were eventually acquired by the Fenwick family's famed stud at Johns Island, near Charleston.

In the years which followed the Revolution, Americans were on

The good manners and the sunny disposition of the Quarter Horse make him an ideal mount for younger riders. This six-year-old rider seems quite secure on her full-grown Quarter Horse, probably more secure than she would be on an ill-tempered pony.

the move westward. During the late 1770s and early 1780s, more than a hundred thousand pioneer families, from New England all the way to the far south, packed up their belongings and joined in the big push into the virgin frontier lands. The poorest of the migrants carried their worldly goods on their backs. The more prosperous had hitches of oxen, horses, or mules. But for all, the hope that lay ahead was for a new and better life in the fertile expanses that lay beyond the Appalachians.

Most especially was this true of the settlers who came from the South. Though the nation had become, in name, a free republic, true "democracy" was practiced far more widely in the North than in this part of the country. More than ever, the society of the southeastern seaboard was dominated by the "haves," with their elegant town houses in glittering centers that stretched from Baltimore to Charleston, and their vast tobacco and rice plantations.

Increasingly, too, did the Southern "nobility" come to depend upon African slaves as the primary source of both farm and domestic labor. The economic and social conditions in the early days of the pre-Civil War South gave little promise for self-advancement to the poorer classes of white farmers and trappers. And though incredible hardships lay in store for them in the wilderness to the west, there was always the chance for a better future than they could possibly attain in a part of the country where Independence, instead of bringing greater freedom, had done nothing more than advance the already well-entrenched cause of feudalism.

At this time, the Commonwealth of Virginia still laid claim to the vast, unsettled territory of Kentucky, which had been explored a decade earlier by Daniel Boone and John Finley. Now this virgin land was to become the principal objective of many of the pioneer families from the south. Many Quarter Horses accompanied the stream of settlers, which soon was pouring through the Cumberland Gap into Kentucky and southern Ohio, as saddle, pack, and wagon animals. Once the pioneers reached their homesites, these horses were put to work pulling stumps and towing plows, earning their meager keep at tasks which, as horseman and writer Nelson Nye aptly points out, "no Thoroughbred could have stood up to." The tough Chickasaw element in his background was once again standing him in good stead, and, to quote Nye again: "Out in the brush, he became a race horse again."

As it had been in the early days of the Tidewater, dense forests prevented end-to-end distance racing (even if the poor settlers had been able to lay hands on any of the costly blood horse stock). So quarter racing, ever close on the heels of the moving frontier, became one of the main amusements of the pioneers.

There is today a sign on South Broadway, in Lexington, the hub of the Kentucky "blue grass" country, which reads: "First race course—Near this spot pioneers in 1780 established the starting point of the first race path in Kentucky, extending southward one quarter mile." Shortly thereafter, a similar race path was hacked out of the brush at Shallowford Station, on the old Boonesborough-Harrodsburg pike.

Not the least of the perils which confronted the early settlers in Kentucky was that posed by extremely hostile Indians. Actually, Kentucky had a rather small permanent Indian population. But the land was rich in game, particularly in the highly prized buffalo, and Indian tribes from neighboring territories sent frequent hunting parties into this area. They were fiercely resentful of the white intruders and made countless hit-and-run attacks on the early settlements.

One of these was to play a dramatic part in the outcome of an early quarter race held in 1783 at the Shallowford Station path. The winner was just bounding over the finish line when an Indian stepped from behind a cane thicket and put an arrow through his heart.

Much of the same sort of atmosphere that prevailed around the early Maryland and Virginia quarter races clung to the sport as it moved westward. There was the usual heavy consumption of strong drink and the consequent bickering and brawling over results of races. William T. Porter, in his celebrated account called "Quarter Race in Kentucky," describes one such disputed finish in which a "dozen men were produced, who were ready to swear that gimlet-eye [the judge] was drinking a stiff cock-tail at the booth and was on the far side of it when the horses came out, and consequently must have judged the result through two pine planks an inch thick."

In another Kentucky quarter race between a horse and a mare, as reported in *The Spirit of the Times,* the correspondent observed that one of the judges was "so cross-eyed he could see his own head." As the race ended, this reporter wrote, "all hands made for the winning post. Here I heard 'mare's race!'—'No she crossed over the horse's path'—'The boy with the shirt rode foul!' " After much squabbling, the result was declared a dead heat. Then the judges reversed themselves and said that the horse had won by ten inches. One of them, the correspondent noted, had by this time become "so angered that he had gone home."

Quarter racing of the late eighteenth and early nineteenth centuries was by no means confined to Kentucky. The research of Robert Denhardt and others reveals it was also much in vogue in Ohio, where regular meetings were held in Cincinnati, Chillicothe, Dayton, and Hamilton; and in Michigan, where tracks were established at Detroit, Adrian, Cold Water, Kalamazoo, Marshall, and Jackson. Both of these states were then, and remain today, important Quarter Horse breeding centers.

The sport also popped up early in the frontier history of states to the south of Kentucky. In a letter to a New York sporting journal, a Mr. Free, of Possum Knob, Tennessee, describes in some detail quarter meetings held at the nearby Stock Creek Paths. In one of the more noteworthy of the events held there, according to Mr. Free, "F. K's Little Breeches" beat "W.R.B.'s Brown Mary." Mr. Free does not report the actual time of the winner in this contest but he does note that the race had started and finished before a visiting Hoosier had time to toss off a dram of whiskey.

In another such notice, this one from a Mississippi gentleman who signed himself "Obe Oilstone" and elected to write his report in rustic dialect, the high point of one quarter meeting was Obe's winning a coveted jacket with red and green stripes all over it, "which I've wore reglar ever Sunday to meetin' ever since I won it."

In another important way the Quarter Horse was now earning his keep in a big way. This was in his role as a stock animal. The raising of cattle became one of the earliest pursuits of the frontiersmen as civilization inched its way westward. But actually, ranching as practiced in the western states had preceded the Revolution by more than a half century.

In *The Horse in America,* Robert West Howard writes of the origin of "cow pens" of a sort that resembled in every particular those which were later used on the cattle spreads of the west. The first of these, Howard tells us, was erected in 1710 at the fall line of the Savannah and Pee Dee rivers, in the Georgia–South Carolina area. "The technique used for stocking a cow-pen was," he says, "similar to the one used by Texans 175 years later when they herded feral long horns out of the chaparral for the trail drives to Kansas.

"A troop of horsemen, armed with bullwhips and guns, encircled a feral horse or cattleherd from downwind, then 'worked' it toward the cow-pen and a V-shaped fence that opened, at the point of the V, into a stout, high-walled corral."

This technique, Howard concludes, "obviously depended on superior horsemanship" and "the use of horses that could 'start off like jack rabbits' and 'stop on a two-bit piece!'" Indeed, it can safely be said that today's best stock horses owe a greater debt than many realize to these equine ancestors who served as the cow ponies of the stockmen in the east, starting many years before the Declaration of Independence.

In colonial times stock was handled much as it is today—by superior horsemen mounted on horses that could "start off like jack rabbits and stop on a two-bit piece"; in other words, by men on Quarter Horses.

The Melting Pot

The modern stud book issued by the American Quarter Horse Association lists 24 sire lines which can be considered "sufficiently strong to be classed as families." Eleven of these were established in Colonial times or immediately thereafter, and as noted earlier, the blood of Janus, who was so frequently bred back to his own daughters and grand daughters, dominates this first group of families to the extent that he appears in all but two.* These were the lines established by Lee's Mark Anthony in 1767, and Goode's Brimmer in 1787.

In the later period after the revolution, three more "founding fathers" of the modern breed made their bow. The first of these was a chestnut Thoroughbred named Copperbottom (1828–1860), a son of Sir Archy, the first great "native" American race horse, out of a mare by Buzzard. His dam, incidentally, traced twice to Janus. Copperbottom was bred in Lancaster, Pennsylvania, and was later acquired by Sam Houston who stood him for some 20 years at various East Texas localities. His numerous descendants were noted for their speed, and his line was preserved carefully enough so that his name is still found in many modern breeding charts. After Copperbottom, there was a half century interval in which the Quarter Horse had to get along without the aid of the Thoroughbred. And, as Denhardt points out, this is the "period that is the hardest for the Quarter Horse historian to unravel as once the break with the Thoroughbred was complete, official and reliable records almost cease."

This problem arises immediately in the pedigree of the second sire of a family to appear in this period. This stallion was Shiloh (1844–1869). Shiloh was by Union, a horse five generations re-

* The families tracing to Janus, other than his own tribe, are those of Peacock (1764), Babram (1770), Bacchus (1778), Celer (1780), Twigg (1782), Printer (1804), Whip (1809) and Tiger (1816).

69

moved from Sir Archy, the only registered Thoroughbred to appear in his background on the sire side. The breeding of his dam, Shiloa, is unknown. Shiloh was bred in Tennessee and was brought to Texas by one Jack Batchler. Standing at various places in Texas, most notably around San Angelo, Shiloh was to father a number of highly regarded "short horses" and brood mares.

The third in this trio of pre-Civil War family fathers bears a name that was to become legendary in the entire frontier land of the Southwest. This was Steel Dust (1845–1874). So many and so great were the fine sons and daughters of this stallion that his fame in the stud was very nearly his own undoing. Over a period of years, horses that contained not a drop of Steel Dust's blood were passed off as "Steeldusts." As a matter of fact it is now considered likely that there may also have been several other stallions, not related to him, that were called Steel Dust. As Denhardt says, "Steel Dust would turn over in his grave if he knew how many broomtails were sold under his name." (This counterfeiting reached such a point that the historian and novelist, Phil Stong, in his *Horses and Americans,* commented that "there was not a saddled maverick under a cowhand that was not a Steeldust or you fought the owner.")

The diligent research of the American Quarter Horse Association, conducted by Helen Michaelis, Denhardt, and others, has weeded out many of the phonies, but there is still a sizeable area of confusion in certain other pedigrees.

Equally confused is Steel Dust's own breeding. He was purchased by his owner, Middleton Perry, in Illinois and was brought to stand in Lancaster, Texas. It was represented to Perry that he was a son of a stallion named Harry Bluff, a horse who, like Shiloh, was rather distantly related to Sir Archy. The Quarter Horse stud book accepts Harry Bluff as the sire, "from the information at hand," though it relates another version ascribing him to a stallion named Little Joe out of a mare named Katrina (both untraced), to underscore the official uncertainty over his sire lines. Even less is known of the dam. She was commonly believed to have been of cold-blooded stock. Steel Dust himself is described as a dark bay about 14.2 hands in height. But here too, there is a discrepancy since some versions have run him all the way up to 16 hands.

Besides the families of Copperbottom, Shiloh, and Steel Dust, there is another clan, founded in 1866, the year after hostilities between the North and South had ended, which should probably

Due to selective breeding, which has fixed his characteristics, and to the rise in his popularity, the registered Quarter Horse has become, next to the racing Thoroughbred, the most expensive horse in America. The bidding at this auction at the B. F. Phillips ranch in Texas is as spirited as any at the great Thoroughbred auctions.

be included as belonging to this period in the Quarter Horse's development. This is the family of Billy.

Billy is interesting in that he was the first father of a family to be foaled in Texas, the state which can truly lay claim to being the modern "home of the Quarter Horse." Billy's breeding unites the qualities of the last two mentioned founding fathers. His sire was Shiloh; his dam was Ram Cat, a daughter of Steel Dust. Using Billy as a stud on his good brood mares Paisana and Belton Queen, his owner, W. B. Fleming, of Belmont, produced a clan that enjoyed great popularity in its day and can be found in the pedigrees of every modern strain of Quarter Horses.

In the time immediately following the Civil War, the westward thrust of the nation, which had been blunted by the conflict, was resumed with new vigor. What had been before but a comparative trickle now turned into a flood of new settlers spilling out onto the great plains and prairies of the Southwest. With the construction of rail lines, ranching to supply meat for the markets of the East became a major occupation in this part of the expanding republic. And, as the great cattle empires came into being, there came also the demand for more and better horses.

At this time, the plains still abounded in vast herds of mustangs. Some of these animals were scrubby and, while they made hardy little cow ponies, there were not too many that were suitable for breeding purposes. But, nevertheless, there were some which had retained a good part of the quality which had originally been imported in the ships of the Spanish. Toughened as they had become to the hard life and slim fare of the praries, they proved, when mated to stallions of some blooded background, to be ideal breeding stock for ranch horses. (This practice, as we have noted earlier, probably resulted in some reduction in size and speed, while at the same time it greatly sharpened the inbred "cow sense" found in the Quarter Horse of today.)

It was not by any means only to pure Thoroughbred stallions that the better grade of Spanish mares were bred to improve the quality of the stock horse type. There is no question that there was some infusion of the Morgan, that sturdy little New Englander who had shown his mettle in the Civil War. There is also evidence that Standardbred blood, particularly in Oklahoma, entered the Quarter Horse background during this period. Captain King, founder of the famous ranch that bears his name, not only experimented with Thoroughbreds, Standardbreds, and Morgans in crossings on his band of good Spanish broodmares, but also took an occasional flyer with Arabian and American Saddle Horse stallions as well.

Indeed, Captain King and the Klebergs who followed him at King Ranch were not only themselves very much in the foreground in developing the modern Quarter Horse but their breeding practices were typical of those being carried on by others instrumental in creating the breed of today.

During this later evolutionary stage of Quarter Horse development, breeders like King directed their breeding programs at producing the best possible stock horses regardless of what blood lines were required to accomplish that purpose. J. K. Northway, in an appendix written for Tom Lea's *The King Ranch*, states that this had been King's objective from the outset.

In the late 1860s, he had secured Thoroughbred stallions from the Kentucky "blue grass," paying as high as a thousand dollars, then a very high price, for an individual. These he bred to selected Spanish mares. The cross was found to produce a Quarter type horse of excellent conformation, speedier and nearly a hand taller than its Spanish forbears.

After King's death, Robert J. Kleberg, Sr., continued the program. Eventually, the King Ranch horsemen came to the discovery that, while the first and second crosses on the Spanish mares in King's day had produced superior stock animals, the further introduction of Throughbred and Standardbred blood "did not, on the average, improve the horses as cow horses. In fact, the contrary was true," Northway says. "Many were too big and leggy for ranch work."

When a breeding establishment reaches this sort of impasse, it looks for a stallion like Janus of old, or like the fabulous Steel Dust, whose prepotency in the stud is such that he will stamp his best characteristics on his offspring for many generations to come.

Such a stallion King Ranch finally found in Old Sorrel, an animal which, at the urging of Robert Kleberg, Jr., was acquired by the enterprise in 1916 from George Clegg, of Alice, Texas. When broken to stock work, Old Sorrel soon proved to be the finest cow horse the ranch had ever owned, and it was his owners' hope that he would prove equally successful in the stud.

Many years later in an article prepared for the August, 1946, *Journal of Heredity*, Kleberg and A. O. Rhoad, wrote: "The first constructive effort made in this direction was to breed Old Sorrel to fifty of the best handling and riding mares on the ranch. These

Jane Mayo, three-times World Barrel Racing Champion, on her Quarter Horse, V's Sandy. Everything about this horse spells alertness.

Dean Oliver roping a calf with the aid of his registered Quarter Horse, Trapper. (Photo DeVere)

Walt Linderman bull-dogging off his Quarter Horse, Scotty. These two horses (the white horse is called a "header") know exactly what they are doing. (Photo DeVere)

mares were in most instances of pure Thoroughbred or grade Thoroughbred breeding. The first important effort toward concentrating and preserving his blood was made when Solis, one of Old Sorrel's sons out of a Thoroughbred mare, was mated to one of his daughters from this same band of mares. In the course of a very short time, this band of mares was built up to 35 or 40 in number and in this way Solis was mated to forty of his half sisters mostly from Thoroughbred mares."

Other breeding experiments were made involving Old Sorrel himself, and others among his sons, but his qualities appear always to have been best transmitted through Solis. In the writers' words: "They were fully aware that not every sire has a balance of genetic qualities that will stand the test of close inbreeding without disaster." But the results obtained by mating Solis to the daughters of Old Sorrel "were so good that the management decided to try to perpetuate Old Sorrel through line breeding and inbreeding." How well this formula succeeded was demonstated when Wimpy, a son of Solis and a double grandson of Old Sorrel, in 1941 was awarded the honorific number "one" in the stud book of the newly organized American Quarter Horse Association.

❋   ❋   ❋

In the years between the Civil War and World War I, while King and other prominent ranchers were at work developing what would eventually be the finest breed of stock-handling horse in the world, quarter racing had wended its way into the western plains and mountains.

The wealth to be derived from ranching was not the only lure that drew new settlers west. In 1850, a small party of displaced Indians moving toward California discovered traces of gold not far from Denver, Colorado. Eight years later a larger prospecting group of white men built the first profitable placer-mining plant and touched off the great gold rush. Within a few short years, Denver, Central City, Black Hawk, Golden, and a number of other boom towns blossomed in the Rocky Mountain mining region. Then silver, and finally, in the 1880s, iron, were also found in the Colorado "treasure chest."

For the cowpokes and miners alike, quarter racing became a favorite payday pastime. The first track built in Colorado was in Denver. It was a straightaway of half a mile located at the site where Broadway crosses Cherry Creek. As elsewhere, the races which were run here were marked by rowdyism and, not infrequently, gun fighting.

Writing in a recent issue of *The Cattleman*, Marguerite Riordan described the social conditions of the times: "In those days all roads led to Denver City for the mines were booming. The miners made the money but the cowmen fed them, and the cow waddies brought the beef to market. Consequently, the visiting cowboys were separated from their money with promptness and dispatch."

This was mainly accomplished by the professional gamblers and card sharps who turned up in considerable numbers in the wake of the gold rush to reap a rich harvest of "easy pickin's" from cowpokes and miners alike.

Miss Riordan quotes a horseman of the day as saying: "It did not matter whether it was a horse race or a prize fight, one could always find backers. The promoter of any kind of a match could raise $500 within an hour from the boys in chaps, merely by standing on a street corner and passing the hat. All he had to do was listen to the clink of gold as it fell into his derby."

Quarter racing, a good deal of which was undoubtedly "fixed," was one of the means by which the frontier hustlers tapped the wallets of the hardworking cowpokes and miners.

It is during this period of Quarter Horse development that the breed began to develop the "split personality" that marks it to this day. On one hand, breeding to perfect the working stock horse was the sole objective; on the other, the stress was more on speed than on "cow savvy." In recent years, the Quarter Horse has depended largely on Thoroughbred speed sires to increase his speed. But in this earlier day, quarter racing men couldn't afford to be so fussy about lines. They bred to anything they could find that had speed.

After the establishment of the Billy family, in 1866, the next Quarter Horse tribe to be founded was that of Cold Deck, a son of Old Billy's who was foaled in 1868. Cold Deck, a deep sorrel who stood barely 15 hands, was said to have been bred by one Tom Martin of Kyle, Texas, and was out of a Missouri-bred mare named Maudy. At least that is the official version. Denhardt notes, however, that there is a good possibility this stallion was actually foaled in Missouri and was a son of Steel Dust. He tells an amusing story of how Cold Deck got his name.

According to this version, Steel Dust's owner was out of town, having left instructions with the groom that no one should bring a mare to Steel Dust's court while he was away. The groom, however, got into a poker game in which he was wiped out. In order to refinance his play, he is said to have allowed Steel Dust to be bred to an unidentified mare. The groom's bad luck at cards earned the foal which resulted from this mating the name of "Cold Deck," a gambler's term for a pack of cards that is running against him.

So fast was Cold Deck that his owner, Foss Barker, had a sign hanging on his barn that read: "Cold Deck Against the World." And, as Denhardt puts it, "So many people were ready to put money on Cold Deck that they would run him for a 'nip of corn' or $10,000."

Chronologically, the next founder of a Quarter Horse family was Roan Dick by Black Nick. Roan Dick (1879–1901) spent his racing and breeding days in the state of Illinois and is best remembered for his famed son, Bob Wade, who set a record for the quarter-mile that was not lowered for many years. This family has today been largely absorbed by other strains.

Roan Dick was followed by a stallion described in the Quarter Horse Stud Book as having "contributed more to present-day Quarter Horses than any other horse of his day." This was Lock's Rondo (1880–1897), a chestnut son of Whalebone by Old Billy, out of a Shiloh mare. Rondo stood for many years at the W. W. Lock ranch, near Kyle, Texas, and while very fast himself, he is best remembered for his many swift offspring whose breeding abilities were so strong that it is doubtful this family will ever be wholly submerged into other clans.

After Lock's Rondo, comes Traveler, a mystery animal, about whom more yarns have been spun than any other Quarter Horse in the history of the breed. Many of these tales bear an odd resemblance to the old legends about the Godolphin Barb, who was said to have been originally the gift of a North African potentate to the King of France. Because of his over-spirited ways, the story goes, the Godolphin found no favor in the French court and was found by a kind-hearted English visitor pulling a coal wagon through the streets of Paris. This gentleman, according to the legend, purchased the horse who eventually wound up in the stud of the Earl of Godolphin and lived on to establish the Matchem line of Thoroughbreds.

Unhappily for the partisans of this fantasy, accurate historians have stripped the Godolphin fable of much of its authenticity. But that which envelopes Traveler apparently has considerable substance in fact.

Traveler, whose breeding is wholly untraced officially, is said by some to have been bred in Kentucky and to have been won in a dice game by a building contractor in Eastland County, Texas. Traveler was put to work pulling an earth scraper on the Texas Pacific Railroad line. Ed Bateman, a well-known writer on Quarter Horses who has devoted a great deal of research to Traveler, has said that he was even then an "aged" horse, "if not already smooth-mouthed," and had never been broken to the saddle.

Something about Traveler caught the interest of one of the sub-contractors on the job, who was called "Triggerfoot" Self. Triggerfoot swapped the contractor a mule for Traveler and then drove the latter off to his home in Baird, Texas, between the shafts of a wagon. Triggerfoot must have been a better than average judge of horse-flesh, because no sooner had Traveler been broken to the saddle (by all accounts this wasn't easy because the old boy didn't take at all kindly to being ridden) than he was matched against a fleet quarter mare named Mayflower, whom he roundly trounced.

Never in the memory of any old-timer around Callahan County was Traveler ever beaten. Nor did he ever taste defeat when later he passed to the ownership of Brown Seay and took on the best Quarter Horses in the Lone Star State. His record in the stud was just as phenomenal. It has been said by some critics that the quality of his offspring depended more on the fine mares to which he was bred than upon his own virtues as a stallion. However, this has been stoutly denied by his defenders.

Bateman gives a good illustration of what the old sorrel stud horse could do even when bred to a very ordinary mare. In fact, the mare he cites as an example was a common old beast who pulled the ice wagon in Baird. From this humble lady, Bateman says, Traveler got three illustrious sons: Judge Thomas, who held the world's record for the 3½ furlong distance for some 25 years; Judge Welch, who ran just as well as Judge Thomas, though his best times were not officially clocked; and a polo pony named Buster Brown who went East and was said to have been the best of his day at that vigorous sport.

Three other Quarter Horse families were established before the turn of the century. These were the families of Sykes and Fred and Peter McCue. The Sykes line was created in 1891 by Sykes Rondo (1887–1907). Sykes Rondo is often confused with Lock's

Rondo, mentioned earlier, though their families are quite separate strains. This stallion was a grandson of Old Billy, on the sire side. Grasshopper, his dam, had an untraced pedigree but it was commonly thought that she descended remotely from the old Tiger line which sprang from the stock of Janus.

The family established by Fred in 1897 is most numerous around the state of Colorado, where he was taken from his foaling place in Springfield, Missouri, by his owner, Coke T. Roberds, a notable Quarter Horse man in that Rocky Mountain state. Old Fred (1893–1915) was likewise a grandson of Old Billy, in his case on both sides of his breeding chart.

When they get to discussing Peter McCue, Thoroughbred and Quarter Horse men often get to the point of slipping off their jackets and stepping outside—or almost, anyway. For around this horse rages a controversy that has had horsemen hot under their collars for decades. And it is not one that is likely ever to be solved either.

The Thoroughbred people say flatly that Peter McCue was of their breed. The Jockey Club's records indicate that he was bred by Samuel Watkins, of Petersburg, Illinois, and that he was the bay son of a Thoroughbred stallion named Duke of the Highlands out of a Thoroughbred mare, Nora M. Indeed, Sam Watkins did register his foal as a Thoroughbred with the newly formed Jockey Club in New York. Milo Burlingame, who, it is said, rode him to 14 victories in as many starts, at distances from a quarter-mile up to five and a half furlongs* and later became his owner, substantiated this version of his breeding, and many say that Milo, one of the most able horsemen of his time, knew Peter McCue as well as anyone who ever lived.

The contention of the Quarter Horse people—at least most of them—is that Peter McCue was sired by a Quarter Horse stallion named Dan Tucker. They have signed affidavits attesting to this fact. One of these affidavits was given by Sam Watkins' son, Walter. The reason why, according to this side of the story, Peter McCue was registered as a Thoroughbred was to make him eligible to compete at Thoroughbred tracks. Most Quarter Horse authori-

---

* At least some of the 14 victories alluded to here must have been at unrecognized meetings. Running officially as a Thoroughbred, Peter McCue's record shows that he won only a lifetime total of 10 races, eight of them when he was a two-year-old and had a brilliant season that saw him out of the money only five times.

Taking off at top speed, running flat out, and then stopping on a dime is a specialty of the Quarter Horse. No other breed could make a showing in rodeo events such as calf roping, shown here.

ties accept the dam, Nora M, as being a full Thoroughbred, by Voltigeur; however, Walter Watkins cast some doubt on that too. In a breeding chart which he prepared for publication in the *Quarter Horse Journal,* he shows the parentage of her dam, Kitty Clyde, as "unknown" on both sides. (According to the Jockey Club's records, she was descended from the very famous Maria West family of Thoroughbred mares which traces to Janus).

Thoroughbred or Quarter Horse, Peter McCue was to leave an impact on both families. In the American Stud Book, he is represented by a score of established brood mares. His effect on the Quarter Horse family, though, has been by far the greater, since he is accepted as one of the most significant of the more recent foundation sires.

The remaining two families in the Quarter Horse stud book are those established in 1900 by the Blake horses, and in 1911 by Old Joe Bailey. The so-called "Blake horses," developed in Pryor, Oklahoma, by Coke S. Blake, one of the best-known of all Quarter Horse breeders, are a strain which blends such traditional lines as those of Steel Dust, Shiloh, and the earlier Brimmer. They made their most important mark in racing in Oklahoma, Arkansas, Missouri, and Kansas.

The tribe descended from Old Joe Bailey, and known as the Joe Bailey family, came into being four years after Old Joe Bailey first glimpsed light in the Texas town of Weatherford (a locality later to become perhaps better known as the birthplace of singing star Mary Martin). Old Joe Bailey was bred by Dick Baker. He was a son of the good Quarter Horse sire Eureka out of a mare named Susie McQuirter. As the Quarter Horse Stud book comments, "The Joe Bailey family is the most recent Quarter Horse strain and in all probability will remain more or less distinct."

The Quarter Horse Today

By 1940, some 300 years had elapsed since the days of the quarter running horse in the colonial Tidewater. Since those remote beginnings, the older sire lines had gradually been absorbed into newer families and fresh blood had been introduced from numerous sources until, wholly without over-all supervision, a type was evolved which, when bred back to its own kind, was able faithfully to produce offspring in its own image. When this occurs, a "breed" is created.

With the Quarter Horse, no one could say with any degree of certainty just when this took place, for it was not until this late year of 1940 that any formal organization was put together to establish a registry and publish a stud book. As Garford Wilkinson, writing in the September, 1965, issue of *The Cattleman,* put it: "The early western horseman's lack of interest in a breed registry is understandable. Neither time, nor inclination nor circumstances in the range country were conducive to an organization devoted to recording the ancestry of a horse. Cattlemen knew the type of horse they needed; they bred with a definite purpose."

But with the rapid mechanization of American agriculture in full swing across the nation, leading stockmen and Quarter Horse lovers began to worry that their good stock horse breed would be totally obliterated. The first rancher to advocate a formal registry of this "all-American" breed was, oddly enough, a native-born Englishman, the late Billy Anson, of Christoval, Texas. Anson died before his dream came to fruition. But new advocates of a Quarter Horse stud book came forward. Outstanding among them were Jack Casement, of Sterling, Colorado, and Professor Robert Denhardt, of Texas A&M University, who would later become the American Quarter Horse Association's first secretary as well as one of the breed's leading historians.

The Association's organization, which resulted from a meeting held in March of 1940, at Fort Worth, Texas, was in a sense an outgrowth of another horse group. This was the Texas Palomino Association, a body established two years earlier for the purpose of maintaining a registry of the "golden horses." Prominent among its members were Roy Davis, of Big Spring Texas, who is now editor of the *Quarter Horse Journal,* and a number of other leading Texas horsemen, including Howard Cox, of San Angelo; W.B. Mitchell, of Marfa; Rudolph Swenson, of Stamford; and R.L. Underwood, of Wichita Falls.

The close relationship between the palomino devotees and the Quarter Horse advocates was perfectly natural in view of the fact that it is in the Quarter Horse family that the palomino coloration most commonly occurs.

Meeting in Abilene, Davis, together with Denhardt and Underwood, decided the time was ripe to bring together the various elements who were interested in establishing a registry of Quarter Horses (or "Steeldusts" as they were then rather commonly called, in honor of that great sire).

Early preliminary discussions were held in Fort Worth, following the Southwestern Exposition and Fat Stock Show held there in 1939. These talks led to the larger meeting in 1940 in which some 75 persons participated. This was when The American Quarter Horse Association was formed to "collect, record, and preserve the pedigrees of Quarter Horses in America; to publish a stud book and registry and to stimulate any and all matters such as may pertain to the history, breeding, exhibiting, publicity, sale or improvement of this breed in America." An initial offering of 800 shares of stock in the non-profit corporation was immediately over-subscribed.

From such modest beginnings sprang an organization which was to become the largest of its kind in the world. Today, less than 30 years later, the American Quarter Horse Association, with more than 40,000 members, has registered over half a million horses, and, at its permanent headquarters in Amarillo, Texas, gives full-time employment to some 150 persons, including staff men on the Association's official publication, the *Quarter Horse Journal.*

Not the least of the reasons underlying the phenomenal growth of the Quarter Horse movement, and one which assures its even greater expansion in the future, has been the imaginative program that the Association has directed at the youth of the nation through its sponsorship of shows (including the donation of handsome

The American Quarter Horse Association's administration building in Amarillo, Texas. The statue is of Wimpy P-1, the first horse registered in the Quarter Horse Stud Book. (American Quarter Horse Association)

trophies) and through the free instructional material and motion picture films it furnishes to such groups as the 4-H and the Future Farmers of America.

The great versatility of the Quarter Horse can be seen in the wide range of events in which boys and girls may compete: calf roping, cutting, reining, barrel racing, pole bending, jumping, Western pleasure, Western riding, breakaway roping, stake racing, jumping, showing at halter, and showmanship at halter. Indeed, it is rather a delightful irony that the horse that was so valued by that once-upon-a-time brand of cowboy—lonely, grizzled, flat broke, often a trifle ripe to the nostrils and occasionally given to warming the air with an earthy string of oaths—is now a major influence in developing the healthy character, integrity, and devoted interest in horseflesh of our current younger generation.

While many of the AQHA show classes open to youngsters virtually duplicate the basic stock horse contests that have traditionally aroused pulsating excitement and a born-in-the-blood love of horses among adults, two events are specifically geared to encourage the participation of young people in horse show activities. One of these is the equitation division in which the rider, not the horse, is under the scrutiny of the officials and is judged on seat, hands, and the ability to control and effectively show the horse. The class performs at the walk, jog, and lope and then, in individual turn, the contestants may be asked to articulate figure 8's, gallop on and come to a halt, mount and dismount, and other routines decreed by the officials. Clearly under the terms of such a class a rider will enhance his showing if he has a horse that is a calm, obedient, responsive mount, and consideration is certainly given to the suitability of horse to rider. But the results of the horse's performance are not as important as the methods used by the rider in obtaining them. Thus, a poor rider perched atop a "machine" cannot outplace a good rider whose horse may not be such a push-button ride—a necessary and fair approach, since the young expert rider cannot always afford the most expert horse.

Showmanship at halter is another class specifically devised to invite the enthusiasm of youngsters, to train them in the techniques of showing stock to best advantage, and to encourage those whose own ability may exceed that of the material they have to work with. In showmanship at halter classes the quality of the horse does not count at all in the scoring, and the animal is there "merely as a prop to show the ability of the showman," as the

The Quarter Horse's incredible balance is shown in this sliding stop negotiated at the New Mexico State 4-H show at Tucumcari.

Reining events put the Quarter Horse through an intricate pattern of stops, turns, and changes of lead.

AQHA puts it. Considered, instead, is the appearance of the horse insofar as the human owner can enhance it. The animal must be in good physical condition and admirably groomed. His coat should be cleaned and well brushed, his tail free of tangles, thinned to trimness, and pulled short to hock length. The fuzzy hair inside the horse's ears should be clipped, as well as his whiskers and the shaggy feathering that may grow along the fetlocks. Tack should show the effects of attention by being clean, polished, and in good repair, and the young exhibitor should be similarly tidy in his own appearance and wear proper, workmanlike Western riding clothes.

Further point score in this event evaluates to what degree the young exhibitor has mastered the principles of showing a horse in hand, rather than under saddle. The showman must lead the horse correctly, holding the shank in the right hand with the loose end coiled neatly in the left, and always stationed at the horse's left side. He should allow sufficient leeway for the horse to move freely and in a straight line when requested to walk or trot, yet not so much that the horse may shamble along loosely or begin to frisk. In posing the horse at a standstill, the showman must be sure the horse is standing squarely on all fours and looks alive and alert. To settle the horse into position, he skillfully manipulates the horse with halter and leadshank, for it is forbidden to tap the horse's feet into place, and excessive fussiness or fidgeting around to make the horse perk up is frowned upon. Throughout the demonstration, the showman should follow the official's instructions courteously and accurately, see that he brings out the best in the horse's conformation and way of going, and be sure that the judge has an unobstructed view of the animal. There is distinct emphasis, too, on the exhibitor's dexterity, politeness, sportsmanship, and poise—virtues that could often bear a little more attention in Eastern shows for young horsemen, where an unexpected defeat has been known to be met with waspish comment.

Aside from open jumping classes which have recently and happily crept into the repetoire of Quarter Horse activities and in which English tack is used, most Quarter Horse show contests on the adult level may be loosely grouped into four categories: halter classes, racing events, general riding and pleasure events, and working classes.

Halter classes, as may be gathered from the preceding discussion of showmanship at halter for youngsters, are events in which the exhibitor shows the horse in hand, not under saddle, using simply a halter and leadshank to pose and guide the animal while displaying the entry's "model" Quarter Horse qualities of conformation and action. The ideal "breedy" look of the typical top-notch Quarter Horse, with its fine, wedge-shaped head, short, stocky body, and hefty, muscular quarters, is the quality best appreciated in these classes. In fact, it is largely in the halter arena that the singular conformation of the Quarter Horse has been refined and perpetuated, and it is often these events that breeders scrutinize most carefully in the never-ending hunt for stud and broodmare prospects as well as working stock.

There has been some contention by quarter racing people that model halter stock breeders have bred too much "beefiness" into the type. The model breeders counter with the charge that the racing people, in infusing great amounts of Thoroughbred blood into the racing lines, are breeding the Quarter Horse look *out* of the type. Fortunately, the common love for this breed surmounts all bickering and both factions enjoy their Quarter Horse specialties their own ways. Indeed it is all the more tribute to the strain that it can embrace the widely differing goals of many horsemen. While the racing enthusiasts can breed to lay on speed, others will preserve the short, tough, muscular build that has traditionally stamped the Quarter Horse and made him ideal for such a multitude of uses.

At most AQHA shows, halter class contests are held for weanlings, yearlings, two-, three-, and four-year-olds and older animals of both sexes. There are also halter classes for geldings and still other events called group classes, in which the produce of a dam or the get of a sire are being judged. In Produce of Dam events, two offspring of either sex born of the same dam are exhibited, and though the dam must be a registered AQHA mare, she need not be present. In Get of Sire classes, three offspring of either sex representing the same registered sire are judged. Mare and Foal classes show mares with foals at their side and it is mandatory for the foal to have been born during the current calendar year. Sire and Get classes require that the sire be shown in the company of two of his offspring whose age may not exceed four years. Another event, called the Exhibitors Group, is a class in which four horses of any age or sex are shown in hand, all of them owned by the same exhibitor.

The racing events that take place in the horse show arena are in no way related to straightaway Quarter Horse racing on the tracks—except in that they are another demonstration of the Quarter Horse's incomparable ability to eat up the ground like a charge of dynamite.

Pole bending is a popular event in which the Quarter Horse is required to negotiate an intricate pattern of obstacles without knocking them over. It is a timed event.

But in the ring he shows as well that he can dart like a waterbug in a dozen directions, stop dead, change gears, pivot 360°, keel to the side 45°, square himself, and bolt headlong for the finish. The racing contests—barrel racing, stake racing, and pole bending—are acrobatics under jet propulsion or, as one old-timer put it, "that moment when a Quarter Horse just plain runs like hell—and does it with all the balance and precision of a tightrope walker who knows no net is down there to catch the pieces."

Stake racing, barrel racing, and pole bending are all timed events in which entries compete in individual turn and are required to negotiate at top speed an intricate pattern of obstacles without knocking them over. In stake racing, the obstacles are simply two stakes placed on the course 80 feet apart which the horse dashes to encircle in a large figure 8. The barrel racing course consists of three barrels placed in a triangular arrangement with the distance along each of the two sides measuring 40 yards while the distance at the base is 35 yards. The entrant circles each, forming a cloverleaf pattern, and then charges about 60 yards to the finish. In the pole bending course the poles are situated a scant 21 feet apart making it a neat trick indeed for any horse to weave in and out in swiftly executed serpentines without dislodging the obstacles.

Western pleasure, riding, and trail horse contests may differ in the routines to be executed but share in common the purpose of determining those animals which exemplify the manners, handiness, and basic good sense desirable in a horse to be used for general riding pleasure or over-all ranch work. Pleasure horse classes require a rather simple demonstration of the horse's ability to walk, trot, and lope on a loose rein without undue restraint or obvious cues from the rider. Deft changes of lead and a spirit of quiet willingness are essential, and the judge is free to demand additional approved routines, to confirm his evaluation of the entry.

The Western riding horse class is, as the AQHA specifies, "neither a stunt nor a race. It is a competition in the performance and characteristics of a good, sensible, well-mannered, free and easy moving ranch horse which can get man around on the usual ranch chores, over the trails, or give a quiet, comfortable and pleasant ride in open country through and over obstacles." The horse is expected to swing into his gaits easily, switch leads with natural responsiveness, stand quietly beneath his rider during the opening and closing of a gate, and handle such minor obstacles as a log or fallen fence that might be encountered along any casual ride. Periodically the

AQHA designates patterns and drills suited for the testing of horses in these events and the illustration below is typical of what an entry may encounter.

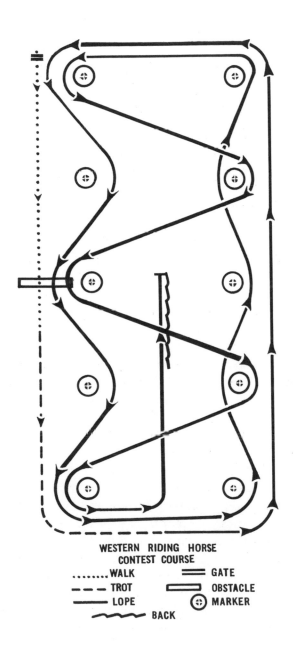

WESTERN RIDING HORSE
CONTEST COURSE

.... WALK   ═══ GATE

– – – TROT   ▭ OBSTACLE

——— LOPE   ⊕ MARKER

〰〰 BACK

Though the initial part of trail horse classes merely tests the entries at a walk, trot, and lope along the rail where the horse is expected to exhibit the characteristics already covered, the latter segment of the contest presents circumstances of a more unusual nature. Hopefully the horse will surmount the obstacles with flying colors, accepting each and readily following his rider's bidding. A typical routine in this class will include such tests as: opening, passing through, and closing a gate; riding over at least four logs; riding over a wooden bridge; sending the horse freely into a trailer. Optional obstacles range from negotiating a water hazard or hobbling the horse to mounting and dismounting from either side or simply putting on and removing a slicker.

It is perhaps in the working classes that the Quarter Horse really shows his mettle in a manner fit to awe even the veteran hardcase show-goer. Here he races not against the artificial gamesmanship of the clock, but against the pressures of a true working situation. He sprints and dashes with trip-spring speed, wheels in mid-air, and shudders to a stop not simply to show that he can do it, but because if he doesn't do it—and do it well—both he and his rider will end up in the dust 50 yards from the maverick they're supposed to be after. Such an exhibition may well represent the greatest measure of a horse's intellience quotient yet conceived, for in these events the horse must react on his own impulse to handle any circumstance that a calf or steer may present. No memorized ritual—though it may be as dazzling as the feats of the famed Lipizzaners of the Spanish Riding School in Vienna—can substitute for the spontaneous reactions that arise from the horse's own intellect as he seeks to cope with an entirely unpredictable creature in situations impossible to rehearse.

A variety of reining classes, in which the entry does not work with real livestock, gauges the horse's advance preparation for the swift and obedient action that would be required of him in true ranch labor. The intricate stops, turns, and changes of lead, shown in a typical reining course on page 95, commit the horse to judgment based "on the neatness, dispatch, ease, calmness and speed with which it performs the pattern," according to AQHA rules. Marked against the horse are any symptoms of nervousness, recalcitrance, unsureness of foot or disbalance such as opening his mouth to evade the bit, breaking his gaits, failing to change leads, jumping the gun on signals, tripping, stumbling or falling, wringing his tail, bouncing to a stop or skittering into it sideways, and backing askew.

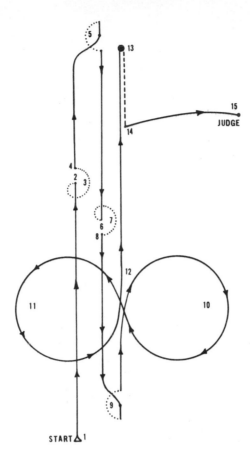

REINING PATTERN

Ride pattern as follows:

1 to 2. *Run at full speed (should be run at least 20 feet from any fence or wall).*

2. *Stop.*

3. *Do a 360-degree spin.*

4. *Hesitate.*

5. *Proceed to the area beyond the end of the arena or plot and do a left roll back over the hocks.*

6. *Stop.*

7. *Do a 360-degree spin.*

8. *Hesitate.*

9. *Proceed to the area beyond the other end of the arena or plot and do a right roll back over the hocks.*

10 and 11. *Ride a figure 8.*

12 to 13. *Run at full speed.*

13. *Stop.*

13 to 14. *Back.*

15. *Walk to judge and stop for inspection until dismissed.*

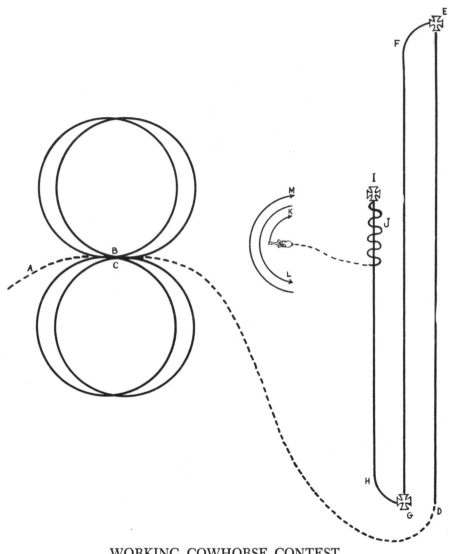

WORKING COWHORSE CONTEST

Rider shall start his workout with a figure 8, executed at a lope two times and of sufficient size to avoid short, choppy turns (A-C). Failure of horse to change both front and hind leads shall be faulted. The smoother and more even the gait, the more credit to the horse.

The entry shall then go to the end of the arena (D), turn and run full length of the arena and make a straight sliding stop (E), turn away from the rail (F), run the full length of the arena and make a straight sliding stop (G), turn away from the rail (H), run to the center of the arena, and make a straight sliding stop (I).

After allowing the horse to gather itself, back the horse in exactly the opposite direction in a straight line for 10 to 15 feet (J).

Horse shall then be brought up to the judge, stopped and, with weight on the hind quarters and with hind legs in position, make a quarter turn to the right (K), half turn to the left (L), and half turn to the right (M). The entry shall then retire from the arena.

Barrel racing has become one of the most popular events in Western horse shows. Only the Quarter Horse, with his early speed, agility, and balance, can manage the course with any speed.

Such common flaws as these are guarded against not only in reining events but are cause for penalty in virtually all working classes where the efficient, businesslike manner of the horse is under consideration. Another customary class in which these values would apply is the Working Cow Horse class. As a preliminary, the entry executes the official Working Cow Horse maneuvers diagrammed on page 96. He then may be called upon to show his skill in herding and turning an actual cow. A single test cow is held in one end of the arena while the horse is allowed to get a good look at it. Then the cow is permitted to run down the side of the arena, during which time the contestant is obliged to turn the cow twice each way against the fence. Then the cow must be herded to the center of the ring and circled once each way.

A multitude of roping classes reveal the spectacular accomplishments of the Quarter Horse when used with lariat to halt the meandering calf or steer. Though all AQHA roping classes are conducted under rodeo regulations (that is, the contestant remains behind a barrier until the released calf or steer has been given a start of a specified distance, and breaking the barrier prematurely or any misconduct behind it is cause for penalty), except for youth breakaway roping, they are not timed as in rodeo events. Time score on the rider's part is not of real concern, but rather the excellence with which the horse engineers his rider into position to make the throw and the diligence with which the horse then keeps the rope taut, facing the calf, so the critter is held secure but not dragged.

Generally, there is an outside limit of two minutes for the rider to effectively show his mount. In some classes, such as calf roping, AQHA rules concede the rider as many throws as necessary within those two minutes. The only stipulation is that if a second rope is thrown, two ropes must be carried so that the first line can be left to drag along the ground demonstrating that the horse is appropriately skilled to handle the dangling hindrance. After completing the catch the rider makes his legal tie binding three legs of the calf above the heel and below the hock in a fashion provably secure.

Team tying is a version of calf roping in which two riders and two horses operate as a team, one pair acting as the heeler and the other as the header. Though they function as a team, and though a horse may be entered as a header or heeler or subsequently both in two go-rounds, the horses are judged on an individual basis and it must be specified beforehand which of the two is being scored.

In team tying, the rider of the heading horse starts behind a bar-

The Quarter Horse is a great scrambler, capable of making amazing recoveries and sparing his rider a bone-crushing fall.

Perfect balance of horse and rider is the key to champion barrel racing form. This young lady and her handsome Quarter Horse are on their way to a winning time in this event. (Photo by Darol Dickinson)

rier and runs to follow the steer. Heelers may or may not be required to start behind a barrier, according to the official's direction. They should cleverly control the steer by following at the heels, enabling the rider to make a throw that will snag the animal by one or both hind legs. The header ropes the steer by the head, of course, and is the one to make the tie.

The announced intention of the horses' positions before entering the ring is the basis on which they will be judged. In other words, they cannot change places in mid-performance. Also, the rider on the horse being scored, whether he's the header or the heeler, has a limit of two loops and must carry his second loop tied to the saddle; he cannot recoil the first. The rider on the unscored horse has unlimited throws. Once again, the principles involved are how handily and effectively the horse sets up his rider for the throw at head or heels, and then how well the horse keeps the quarry steady without dragging or injuring it.

A variation of team tying is the Dally Team Roping event, similar to the former in that both a header and heeler operate together for the benefit of whichever one of them is being scored. Only steers are used in the roping, and after the catches are made, the steer is *not* tied off. Also, though the scored contestant may throw two loops within the two-minute time period, he may carry only one. This is not tied to the saddle horn beforehand but given several quick twists (called "taking the dally") when the catch is made; should the rider miss his throw, he is required to recoil the same lariat. After the ropes are secure at the heel and head, no tie is made; instead the steer is kept immobile by the taut, clever backing action of the horses at either end as they shrewdly watch their prisoner to prevent any surprise moves.

The final event in the array of roping contest is the Dally Steer Stopping class. As specified by the title, here again only steers are used as the roping objects. The dally rope, which is twisted around the saddle horn after the catch rather than affixed previously, is the required piece of equipment. Only two loops within the two-minute time period are permitted. A single horse and rider—not a pair— take the steer, roping him at the head. Thereupon the steer is left untied, but is nevertheless kept helpless but unharmed by the fine holding action of the horse.

Whatever stamps the lion as unmistakable king of the jungle has done the same for the cutting horse at Western shows. The talents of other Quarter Horses at their respective jobs are altogether re-

The performance of the cutting horse represents the closest union of physical agility and mental superiority that exists in any kind of horse. This is the Quarter Horse, Marion's Girl, Buster Welch up. (The Quarter Horse Journal)

markable, and the reigning champions deserve as high a rank among the equine greats as the Kelsos and Man O'Wars. But there is something about the cutting horse that makes his singular performance one of the most electrifying a witness can behold. It is a quality that defies analysis for there is no logical *reason* for the good cutting horse to be any more exciting than a horse that's good at something else. But then there is no logical reason for the Kentucky Derby, which is not the oldest, nor the longest, nor the richest of Thorough-bred races, to be one of the world's most exciting sporting events. A difference nevertheless exists between watching something that is excellent, even perfect, and watching something that simply makes the blood run a little faster. Perhaps the mystery lies in the difference between craftsmanship and art, though the lean straight-forward folk who traditionally ride the cutting horse would be the last to use such hifalutin terms to describe their business. Or per-haps the special value of a cutting horse is that his performance rep-resents the closest union of physical agility and mental superiority that exists in any kind of horse.

The cutting Quarter Horse is, in motion, a precision instrument that *thinks,* and reveals the full measure of his skill not through any fancily contrived "act" but through the self-determined achievement of his purpose: to separate and hold one steer away from the herd of others. As a goal, keeping one steer apart from others may sound pathetically simple, perhaps more so to untutored city-folk who tend to think of all cattle as being stupid, placid, shambling beasts. In fact, the steer is a shifty, lunging, bolting, conniver who will go to any lengths to avoid being separated from his kind, and indeed his des-peration is not without potential menace. There is probably nothing harder to deal with than that combination of orneryness and crafti-ness which is the eternal essence of the steer and always contains possible trouble. This is what the cutting horse must deal with pos-sibly dozens of times in the course of a day's work on the range—or, in the show ring, for a two-and-a-half-minute period which sums up all his brilliance.

From the moment the herd is released in the arena, the cutter selectively eyes one to be diverted and from that moment on his gaze never leaves his charge. Thenceforward, too, the sheer physical mastery of the horse's own body is obvious. The reins are completely dropped on the cutter's neck, for even so much as the slightest cue from the rider is sufficient cause for penalty. A second's loss of ad-vantage over the steer, a single extra stride that would cause him to overrun the critter, a frustrated attempt to corner him against the fence, an accidental switching of the tail to betray the horse's nervousness, an awkward, precipitous move that would completely disrupt the herd while the horse is amid its ranks bringing forth his quarry, an accidental gesture that could injure the flightly maverick —all would justify a penalty and mar a perfect performance. But gently, almost maternally, the cutter ushers his charge away from the bunch, watchful, relentlessly on guard, and equally careful not to harm the steer. The creature, he knows, will instinctively try to drive its way back. But when he plunges, the cutter is there first, racing, feinting, flexing, virtually folding his body in a series of graceful gymnastics that block, turn, and contain the other animal. For one split second he sprints at full throttle, then plants his feet and skids to a dirt-flying stop, shifts his front legs and lowers his dynamic haunches in anticipation of the next wild and vagrant maneuver of the steer. As the expert top hand L. N. Sikes says in his book *Using the American Quarter Horse*, "I've seen a cutting horse down in some awful positions—almost down on the ground spread out like an ink blotter. But it wouldn't make any difference which way the cow went—she was looking right square in that horse's eyes when she stopped."

Sikes' allusion to the cutter's constant watchfulness brings us to the mental quality of the horse's performance. The cutting Quarter Horse does more than just scrutinize the cow. And he has more than the basic "cow savvy" that makes him know, like a mare with her foal, how to nudge and needle another creature along. He possesses a specific awareness of what his cow is going to do before the animal has actually resolved to do it. In a fleeting micro-second that awareness becomes a trigger which not only compels the horse to move but gauges just how far and just how fast, and just what might come next. Part of the spectator's thrill is that he can virtually see this mechanism clicking—and, with all his human senses, is wholly incapable of keeping up with it.

Sikes goes on to observe, "The cutting horse is nearly always a registered Quarter Horse nowadays, and he's been taught his trade so well that lots of old-time cowboys wouldn't believe it unless they could see a modern cutting contest." Here again Sikes hints at a vital point in the making of the cutter, or, indeed, any cow horse—the teaching. Strangely enough, the training of a stock horse represents a reversal of the tendency of our times. In an age where everything from eating to courting is done full steam ahead, the vast majority

The cutting horse never takes his eye off the calf he is separating from the herd. Here the champion War Leo keeps his attention riveted on a particularly stubborn fellow. (Photo by Dalco)

The highly maneuverable yet calm Quarter Horse makes an ideal "pick-up" mount for rodeo bronc busters.

of stock horse handlers take the training process slow and easy. This is certainly different from the methods of a hundred years ago when, as the rest of life rambled along in its own good time, only the horse was broken in haste, initially by drifting bronc-busters, then by overworked ranch hands who had to get as much as they could as fast as they could out of the dozens of horses they dealt with. The rough-and-ready system couldn't have been too bad since it turned out a host of memorable horses among the old timers, and the same principles are, in fact, still employed by Louis Cabrell of Tres Pinos, California, who is one of the top cutting, roping, and reining horse trainers. Cabrell won't even sneeze at a horse until he's four years old. Then, beginning from absolute scratch, he halter breaks the subject in one day—a process that is far from simple, since the willful strength and abject fear of an unhandled four-year-old horse is exceeded only by the determination of Cabrell himself. The next day Cabrell removes a little more of the horse's steam by tying the reins from headstall to tail on each side for an hour. On the third day he hits the saddle and then follows up with three stiff training sessions in the corral. That's all it takes before he heads out to open pasture and begins working the horse with cattle. As a rule, Cabrell turns out a usable cow horse in six months and, if the horse is made of the right stuff, a competition contender within one year.

You can't argue with success—least of all Louis Cabrell's, whose system saves time and expense and has proved its value to highly satisfied owners. Unfortunately, it is a method that may take a little more out of an animal than the farseeing horseman wants—or in its haste may never bring out the full potential of the sleeper, the horse that has the goods and is basically willing to deliver, but simply takes a little longer to come around. It is a process that turns out a multitude of perfectly schooled horses in a minimum of time because it wastes nothing on the whims of an animal's individuality. But it fails to take into account the fact that the difference between the good horse and the truly great horse often *is* individuality, the extra bit of something inside that the horse can draw on when the chips are down. It is the desire to preserve some of this inner substance that prompts most Quarter Horse trainers of today to take the teaching phase slowly and patiently, letting reasonable time be the test that separates the average workers from those of top potential. The outer substance does all right too if the result can be reflected in prices, for cutting horse champions may sell for upwards of $30,000.

At such giant plants as King Ranch in Texas and Sikes' own training stable at Van Alstyne, Texas, and among top trainers like Jack
Elliott of San Benito County, California, and Bob Burton of Arling-
ton, Texas, horses begin their training in earnest generally as late
three-year-olds or young four-year-olds. By this time the horse's
bones are sufficiently developed to take the pounding and jarring of
cutting work, and by this time, too, the pupils have been quietly and
gently broken to saddle, bride, and thorough handling by man.
When an Elliott-trained horse, for example, is first mounted at the
age of two and a half, the horse is so calm and used to being worked
under, over, and around by man he rarely so much as crow-hops.

A major factor in teaching the cutter is the trainer's own shrewdness in judging how far and how fast to bring the horse along, and
how much or how little prompting is required. Discussing his methods in *The Chronicle of the Horse,* Bob Burton says: "I don't work
cattle with a horse every day. That will sour him. And I don't ever
ride him hard. You want a cutting horse to keep a little edge. After
a month of riding I can tell if a horse has the ability or not." He
goes on to caution: "Many horses will start off good then sour out.
For that reason, I like to work a horse a couple of months and then
let him rest for 30 to 60 days. By rest, I mean not work cattle. The
best thing for a horse during this rest period is to be used on a ranch
and get a chance to really stretch and move out. I think rest periods
every so often are necessary for any horse . . . even a finished cutting
horse. Then they're really ready to look at a cow." Burton should
know; he has trained such immortals of cutting horse history as the
incomparable Poco Bueno, Jesse James, and Beaver Creek. He rode
his own mare, Miss Nancy Bailey, to her place among the top 10
cutting horses in the country for five years, and she was named a
World Champion Cutting Horse of the National Cutting Horse Association.

Burton advises starting the horse off working a single cow in a
round or oval arena with no corners where the calf can retreat and
quit. The idea is to get the horse to learn to track and head the cow,
to concentrate on getting the advantage of her, keeping his eyes on
her every moment and resisting any other distraction. After Burton
has had his horse trail the cow around for a while, he turns the cow
into a herd which he keeps in an adjoining pen and lets the horse
bring out another to work in the arena while the bunch remains in
the nearby corral. He repeats the process over and over, with the
horse selecting and returning calves among the bunch until finally

The world champion cutting horse "Cutter Bill" shows just as much class in his everyday farm chores as he does in the show ring. The Quarter Horse is above all else a working horse.

the herd can be moved right into the arena without bothering the horse. Without even knowing it, the horse has been eased into cutting, holding and returning a single cow from the herd, which is exactly what he's supposed to do.

Though methods of cutting cattle have undergone little change in the last hundred years, trainers have not wholly ignored the blessings of the mechanical age. A recent contraption, now coming into wider use, is a simulated automatic steer mounted on wheels and operated by remote control. It works rather like an electric golf cart, but the "driver" operates it from the sidelines. Some ranchers consider it an invention of the devil and admit to a certain timidity when faced with the spinning, spurting antics of the unpredictable contrivance. "It just ain't human," says one rancher. Others find it of great value, declaring that it really teaches a horse to move and gives a little more challenge to the horse who thinks he's so wise and shifty that he can outfox anything breathing. Certainly it must have some advantages, since just such an automatic calf is owned by the Cauble Ranch in Denton, Texas, where Cutter Bill, one of the great cutting horse champions of all time, stands at stud and enjoys occasional matches of wit with the mechanical opponent.

In giving tips to the amateur who may not be equipped with large arenas, holding pens, and electric steers, Sikes warns that many cowmen vow that horses are either born with cow sense or they don't have it, period. Fortunately, when a buyer puts his money on a good Quarter Horse, he stands that much more of a chance of coming up with the element Mr. Sikes speaks of. For one thing, as has been pointed out earlier, horses of eastern Mediterranean origin have been used in variations of bull sporting and cow handling for so long that one suspects that animals of this heritage have acquired some legacy of instinct in the same direction. It is even more certain that horses of oriental blood, such as the Arabian and the Thoroughbred, have a basic sensitivity, a fiery alertness to the world around them that often takes itself out in an almost eccentric interest—occasionally fearful and often affectionate—in all manner of things and creatures surrounding them. Combine this oriental sensitivity with the shrewdness and common sense of range horses on the plains a century and a half ago, and the result is the Quarter Horse—gifted with an innate "intellectual curiosity" by the constantly reinforced presence of eastern blood and the clever knowledge of how to use it born of other ancestors' rugged experience in the wild. When a Quarter Horse takes his first look at cattle he'll probably be inter-

Cutter Bill reacts just as quickly to a mechanical calf used in training cutting horses.

ested if only because he can't stand boredom. And this is the first leg up. In fact, Mr. Sikes submits that the beginning trainer can often get an idea of whether his horse will readily swing into the cutting game just by observing how keen a reaction the horse displays when watching cattle at a distance. In recommending a simple start, he suggests trying the horse at first on an older, slow-moving cow which won't give the horse much trouble. Attempt to keep her away from the herd simply by urging the horse to move when she moves, stop when she stops, and block when she turns. Eventually the horse absorbs the idea that this animal is supposed to be kept out of the bunch.

In order to detect other clues, Sikes rides a horse behind a small bunch of cattle that are moving along. "If he has cow sense, the horse will get to watching them. He may even want to nip at them or he might back his ears at them. . . . If a cow walks or trots from the herd, you'll find the horse wants to go see about that."

While such pointers are unquestionably useful to the beginner, it must also be stressed that a cutting horse can only become as good as the cattle he works with—and the rider who trains him. The horse cannot progress if all he has to cut are lazy, worn out, baggy old she-critters. Nor can he develop the fabulous self-propelled cutting horse initiative if the rider continues yanking at his head and using spur-happy heels beyond the point where the horse really requires guidance. Here, indeed, is an essential difference between the general ranch horse and the cutter. The ranch horse is serviceable because he responds to and depends on signals of rein and leg given by the rider, and he knows his work is done when the reins are finally dropped. The cutter's work *begins* when the reins are dropped. Cues from the rider soon become useless because the better the cutting horse gets, the more jumps he is ahead of his human master. Once the horse knows what is expected, over-prompting, especially at the head, is to be avoided. Otherwise the horse may develop a fear of moving fast lest he be yanked down at the mouth. In fact Bob Burton's observation is that "often the ones that rein good become too dependent on it" to make the best cutters.

In dwelling at length on the training and showing of Quarter Horses in AQHA recognized show contests, there has been no intent to slight the value of Quarter Horses in the hell-for-leather world of rodeo. Here, too, the Quarter Horse emerges as the partner proven superior in all events from fast-paced roping to bone-splitting steer wrestling, a contest in which the horse can actually kill the rider

The Quarter Horse is the king of the rodeo, whether used in roping . . .

in bull-dogging . . .

or in team roping.

if he does not place him in correct position to lunge from the saddle and literally take the bull by the horns. Then the horse must swiftly peel away, allowing the rider ample room to pull his opponent down. In fact rodeo, with annual attendance in recent years approaching the 10 million mark—which surpasses annual American League baseball attendance—has become one of the hottest spectator sports in the country. On the other hand, it cannot honestly be said that rodeo is a brand of sport likely to invite participation by those who have a ranch to run, a job to hold, and a family to feed, since frequent detours to a hospital are commonly necessary. Furthermore, in all forms of rodeo contests it is the rider rather than the horse who is scored, and though the horse is indispensable, he remains a mere shadow behind the rider's glory. Nine times out of ten, however, the rodeo rider's shadow has a generous measure of good red Quarter Horse blood in his veins.

In AQHA show activities, the situation is reversed, for in most classes the horse is the contestant and it is his name that goes on record for having gained the victory. It is much to the credit of the AQHA that it has devised an excellent method of recording the show results of competition horses and evaluating their success. Under this system an official Register of Merit (usually referred to as ROM) has been established which is a kind of achievement roster to which a horse is elevated when he gains a specified number of points that are awarded to him with each show-ring win. The entire scale of points varies with the type of class and how many contenders there are in it. A large class in which there are 28 or more entries is worth 6 points to the winner, 5 for second place, 4 for third, 3 for fourth, 2 for fifth, and 1 for sixth, but a very small class in which there are only four to seven entries is worth just a single point to the winner and nothing to the runners-up. If there are fewer than four entries, no point credits at all are awarded and such classes as Pole Bending, Trail Horse, Western Pleasure, and Western Riding are worth only half-point value. The coveted title of AQHA Champion is bestowed on horses which have amassed a minimum of 30 points in a selected variety of classes and is an even greater distinction than the initials ROM beside a horse's name.

The healthy competition of AQHA-sponsored show ring events and the lively pursuit of ROM honors has done much to bring the modern Quarter Horse close to ordinary everyday horse-loving folk right to the forefront of the sport of kings.

No public competition in the last quarter century—equine or

otherwise—has grown with the raging speed of straightaway Quarter Horse racing. Its current popularity has swept the West like a tidal wave and brought to bear, in states far afield, pressure on legislatures to franchise the sport in their own districts. It is true, of course, that quarter racing never really became extinct. If an owner knows his horse has a drop of Quarter Horse blood in him, there's something about that drop that makes a man want to find out how fast it can take him down the local stretch. Two such men and horses is all it takes to make a race, and there were plenty of these in frontier towns where such legendary heroes as Steel Dust and Traveler are said to have made and broken the betting populace of miners, drifters, cowhands, and railroad builders.

Nor were these contests always rural, vagrant, folksy affairs. Organized tracks existed in the Midwest, and such strongholds as Colorado, Oklahoma, and Texas have traditionally fostered keen-spirited racing competition in the strain. Indeed, numerous sources declare that in Texas, Thoroughbred racing was preceded by Quarter Horse racing and the overwhelming popularity of the latter was not least among the causes that helped to inspire a change of allegiance and encourage that state to become a major producer of the short-distance horse breed.

Despite the enduring loyalty of these constituents, there was a tendency for Quarter Horse racing to be slowly pushed to the fringes of the horse world and for the greater glamor of racing's limelight to fall upon the titans of the Thoroughbred field. In point of fact, in 1945 a dismal total of 25 recognized Quarter Horse races were held, and the future did not look very much brighter when, in 1949, William Kyne, then president of the Bay Meadows track in San Mateo, California, initiated the idea of slipping in a Quarter Horse race as a preliminary to the regular card of Thoroughbred events. The purse was only $400, but where there's a gamble—large or small—there are Quarter Horses, and where there is Quarter Horse racing there are flashing starts, breakneck drives down the fleeting stretch, and nail-biting photo finishes fit to send the racing fan into a fever pitch of enthusiasm. The fever was highly contagious and soon a real demand built up for more of these exciting sprints.

A decade passed as the sport snowballed until in 1962 the year's recognized Quarter Horse races numbered over 2,700. The year's distributed prize money totalled $3,188,410 and the amount bet came to $53,679,106. It is not surprising that 1962 was a landmark in Quarter Horse activity, for one year earlier, in 1961, Quarter

A Quarter Horse being used as a pick-up mount for a rodeo bronc buster.

Horse racing achieved a record by breaking the "money barrier" and offering the richest purse in racing for its All-American Futurity. This single race, covering all of 400 yards, was worth $202,425, as opposed to the Kentucky Derby worth $163,000, the Belmont Stakes worth $148,650, and the Preakness worth $178,700 in the same year. Six years later even this enormous bounty more than doubled with the 1967 purse for the race totalling a fortune of approximately half a million dollars.

To insure its patrons of top-quality sport, the nose-to-nose dashes and hair's-breadth finishes that characterize straightaway Quarter Horse contests, the AQHA racing division has arranged a meticulous and rather complicated systerm of levels and sub-levels based on each entry's track running time at any of the official distances. Standard distances are 220 yards, 250, 300, 330, 350, and 400 yards. Speed ratings rank each horse into a time classification among his equals for each of these measurements. The absolute supreme level is a "TOP AAA" rating. To qualify for this a horse must achieve the lightning time of 12 seconds or better for the 220-yard distance and :13.40 for the 250. Still within this highest level, times of :15.60 and higher qualify for this best grade at 300 yards. At 330 yards, times of :17.00 and better rate top AAA. At 350 yards, this grade is composed of :17.90 and better, while 400 yards takes :20.20 or better. At the full quarter of a mile, top AAA must be run in :22.10 or faster. However, if the horse's time is not quite up to the most liberal allotment in the "TOP AAA" range, then he belongs in the next best division which is the "AAA" level, also indicative of extreme distinction and merit. The fastest qualifying times in the "AAA" level begin at :12.01 for 220 yards, :13.41 at 250, :15.61 at 300, :17.01 at 330, :17.91 at 350, :20.21 at 400, and :22.11 at 440. Sub-groupings within the "AAA" rank similarly increase the time standard until a still lower division is reached—the "AA" level. From there, as the clock allowance expands, the rank decreases, going gradually from the "A" grade straight on down to "D," where qualifying time for 220 yards is :13.01 and for 400 is :24.11. To be eligible for ROM honors, racers must achieve an "AA" rating or better.

In addition to this highly refined system of matching horses with their equals, weight allowance handicapping within each classification further evens the chances for victory among the field of runners.

Clearly with all its financial success, genuine public appeal, and scrupulous organization, Quarter Horse racing has returned to the big-time. It has enlivened our age with a new generation of unfor-

The All-American Futurity, besides being the world's richest horse race, is beginning to attain some of the glamour of its Thoroughbred counterparts. Here screen star Robert Mitchum assists in some of the ceremony.

gettable champions—horses like Go Man Go, Pokey Bar, Tonto Bars Hank, and Kimaleta who may perhaps be destined to take a place beside Steel Dust, Traveler, and Peter McCue. The rebirth has, in effect, brought the breed full circle, restoring it once again to distinction and prominence in the world of racing. Certainly no other strain is more deserving of these rewards, for in surviving a past that was not always glamorous and charitable, the Quarter Horse has become an important part of our own history. He dazzled our forefathers in colonial times, pushed westward with them across a continent, carried their burdens, pulled their wagons, guarded their livestock, and delighted their sporting appetite. In modern times he has brought new dimensions to short-distance racing and magically captivated the world of horse shows and rodeo.

Yet beyond all his public triumphs and the charted records of his feats there lies an even greater value—the quality that is never included in the statistics. This is the Quarter Horse's generosity as a friend—a partner, a sharer, an unstinting giver of his substance for the use and pleasure of his master. In the long run, this may be worth more than speed and skill and beauty combined, and, in a world where real friendship is becoming dearer, it may well be what makes the Quarter Horse the sweeping favorite of all his kind.

Scenes like this are appearing with increasing frequency throughout the nation as families turn to horses as an answer to increased leisure time. Here the J. T. Harris family of Amarillo, Texas, relaxes after an enjoyable afternoon spent with their favorite mount—Dutch Clegg, a Quarter Horse. (American Quarter Horse Association)

Index